AT THE MASTER'S FEET

The VISIONS OF SADHU SUNDAR SINGH

SADHU SUNDAR SINGH

AT THE MASTER'S FEET including THE VISIONS OF SADHU SUNDAR SINGH by Sadhu Sundar Singh

This edition is published by Postomorrow Books of Gresham, Oregon

ISBN-13: 978-0615638775 (Postomorrow Books)

ISBN-10: 0615638775

AT THE MASTER'S FEET

BY SADHU SUNDAR SINGH

TRANSLATED FROM THE URDU BY REV. ARTHUR AND
MRS. PARKER
FLEMING H. REVELL COMPANY
LONDON AND EDINBURGH
1922

NOTE BY THE TRANSLATORS

This little book was published in Urdu in India, where also an English translation was issued.

In the preparation of this translation we have been fortunate in having the co-operation of the Sadhu himself, and in concert with him certain alterations have been made with a view to remove obscurities and give added point and clearness wherever possible. While striving to provide a careful translation, a certain freedom of expression has been made use of wherever necessary, at the same time care has been taken to preserve the true spirit and meaning of the original.

To those who, like ourselves, have had the good fortune to see the Sadhu at his work in India, the whole atmosphere of the book is familiar. In true Oriental fashion one has seen him seated on the ground in the midst of a large number of eager inquirers of both sexes and all classes. His bearing on such occasions one can never forget.

His simplicity and plain common sense often lay open the very heart of a spiritual problem, and his quiet humour raises an occasional ripple of amusement, which again subsides into a feeling of reverence as the deeper significance of his answers makes itself felt.

The man himself, in his own gracious and dignified personality, makes an indelible impression on the mind. He becomes more than a charming memory; he remains as a compelling force in the lives of many who have sat with him at the Master's feet.

This little book goes out as an emanation from a mind chastened and refined by experience and prayerful meditation, and chosen by the Lord of love and mercy to make Him known in life as well as in word.

Arthur Parker
Rebecca J. Parker

PREFACE

The words of Christ--

"Ye call me Master and Lord: and ye say well; for so I am." (John xiii. 13)

"Take my yoke upon you and learn of me . . . and ye shall find rest unto your souls." (Matt. xi. 29)

There is nothing so perfect in the world as to be quite above objection and criticism. The very sun which gives us light and warmth is not free from spots, yet notwithstanding these defects it does not desist from its regular duty. It behooves us in like manner to carry on to the best of our ability what has been entrusted to us, and strive constantly to make our lives fruitful.

When the truths set forth in this book were revealed to me by the Master they deeply affected my life, and some of them have been used by me in my sermons and addresses in Europe, America, Africa, Australia, and Asia. At the request of many friends I have now gathered them together in this little book, and though it is possible that there are defects in setting them forth, I am sure that those who read them with prayer and an unprejudiced mind will benefit from them as I have. It would be impossible for me to set forth these truths that have been revealed to me except in parabolic language, but by the use of parables my task has been made comparatively easy.

It is my prayer that as God by His grace and mercy has blessed me by these truths, so also they may be a blessing to every reader.

Your humble servant,

Sundar Singh

INTRODUCTION

First Vision

Once on a dark night I went alone into the forest to pray, and seating myself upon a rock I laid before God my deep necessities, and besought His help. After a short time, seeing a poor man coming towards me I thought he had come to ask me for some relief because he was hungry and cold. I said to him, "I am a poor man, and except this blanket I have nothing at all. You had better go to the village near by and ask for help there." And lo! even whilst I was saying this he flashed forth like lightning, and, showering drops of blessing, immediately disappeared. Alas! Alas! it was now clear to me that this was my beloved Master who came not to beg from a poor creature like me, but to bless and to enrich me (2 Cor. viii. 9), and so I was left weeping and lamenting my folly and lack of insight.

Second Vision

On another day, my work being finished, I again went into the forest to pray, and seated upon that same rock began to consider for what blessings I should make petition. Whilst thus engaged it seemed to me that another came and stood near me, who, judged by his bearing and dress and manner of speech, appeared to be a revered and devoted servant of God; but his eyes glittered with craft and cunning, and as he spoke he seemed to breathe an odour of hell.

He thus addressed me, "Holy and Honoured Sir, pardon me for interrupting your prayers and breaking in on your privacy; but it is one's duty to seek to promote the advantage of others, and therefore I have come to lay an important matter before you. Your pure and unselfish life has made a deep impression not only on me, but upon a great number of devout persons. But although in the Name of God you have sacrificed yourself body and soul for others, you have never been truly appreciated. My meaning is that being a Christian only a few thousand Christians have come under your influence, and some even of these distrust you. How much better would it be if you became a Hindu or a Mussulman, and thus become a great leader indeed? They are in search of such a spiritual head. If you accept this suggestion of mine, then three hundred and ten millions of Hindus and Mussulmans will become your followers, and render you reverent homage."

As soon as I heard this there rushed from my lips these words, "Thou Satan! Get thee hence. I knew at once that thou wert a wolf in sheep's clothing! Thy one wish is that I should give up the cross and the narrow path that leads to life, and choose the broad road of death. My Master Himself is my lot and my portion, who Himself gave His life for me, and it behooves me to offer as a sacrifice my life and all I have to Him who is all in all to me. Get you gone therefore, for with you I have nothing to do."

Hearing this he went off grumbling and growling in his rage. And I, in tears, thus poured out my soul to God in prayer, "My Lord God, my all in all, life of my life, and spirit of my spirit, look in mercy upon me and so fill me with Thy

Holy Spirit that my heart shall have no room for love of aught but Thee. I seek from Thee no other gift but Thyself, who art the Giver of life and all its blessings. From Thee I ask not for the world or its treasures, nor yet for heaven even make request, but Thee alone do I desire and long for, and where Thou art there is Heaven. The hunger and the thirst of this heart of mine can be satisfied only with Thee who hast given it birth. O Creator mine! Thou hast created my heart for Thyself alone, and not for another, therefore this my heart can find no rest or ease save in Thee, in Thee who hast both created it and set in it this very longing for rest. Take away then from my heart all that is opposed to Thee, and enter and abide and rule for ever. Amen."

When I rose up from this prayer I beheld a glowing Being, arrayed in light and beauty, standing before me. Though He spoke not a word, and because my eyes were suffused with tears I saw Him not too clearly, there poured from Him lightning-like rays of life-giving love with such power that they entered in and bathed my very soul. At once I knew that my dear Saviour stood before me. I rose at once from the rock where I was seated and fell at His feet. He held in His hand the key of my heart. Opening the inner chamber of my heart with His key of love, He filled it with His presence, and wherever I looked, inside or out, I saw but Him.

Then did I know that man's heart is the very throne and citadel of God, and that when He enters there to abide, heaven begins. In these few seconds He so filled my heart, and spoke such wonderful words, that even if I wrote many books I could not tell them all. For these heavenly things can be explained only in heavenly language, and earthly tongues are not sufficient for them. Yet I will endeavour to set down a few of these heavenly things that by way of vision came to me from the Master. Upon the rock on which before I sat He seated Himself, and with myself at His feet there began between Master and disciple the conversation that now follows.

I.
THE MANIFESTATION OF GOD'S PRESENCE

The Disciple,--
O Master, Fountain of life! Why dost Thou hide Thyself
from those that adore Thee, and dost not rejoice the eyes of
them that long to gaze upon Thee?

The Master,--
1. My true child, true happiness depends not upon the sight
of the eyes, but comes through spiritual vision, and depends
upon the heart. In Palestine thousands looked upon Me, but
all of them did not thus obtain true happiness. By mortal eyes
only those things can be perceived that are mortal, for eyes of
flesh cannot behold an immortal God and spiritual beings.
For instance, you yourself cannot see your own spirit,
therefore how can you behold its Creator? But when the
spiritual eyes are opened, then you can surely see Him who is
Spirit, (John iv. 24), and that which you now see of Me you
see not with eyes of flesh, but with the eyes of the spirit. If, as
you say, thousands of people saw Me in Palestine then were
all their spiritual eyes opened, or did I Myself become mortal?
The answer is, No! I took on a mortal body so that in it I
might give a ransom for the sins of the world; and when the
work of salvation was completed for sinners (John xix. 30),
then that which was immortal transfigured what was mortal
into glory. Therefore after the resurrection only those were

13

able to see Me who had received spiritual sight (Acts x. 40,41).

2. Many there are in this world who know about Me, but do not know Me; that is they have no personal relationship with Me, therefore they have no true apprehension of or faith in Me, and do not accept Me as their Saviour and Lord. Just as if one talks with a man born blind about different colors such as red, blue, yellow, he remains absolutely unaware of their charm and beauty, he cannot attach any value to them, because he only knows about them, and is aware of their various names. But with regard to colors he can have no true conception until his eyes are opened. In the same manner until a man's spiritual eyes are opened, howsoever learned he may be, he cannot know Me, he cannot behold My glory, and he cannot understand that I am God Incarnate.

3. There are many believers who are aware of My presence in their hearts bringing to them spiritual life and peace, but cannot plainly see Me. Just as the eye can see many things, yet when someone drops medicine into the eye does not see it, but the presence of the medicine is felt cleansing the inner eye and promoting the power of sight.

4. The true peace which is born of My presence in the hearts of true believers they are unable to see, but, feeling its power, they become happy in it. Nor can they see that happiness of mind or heart through which they enjoy the peace of My presence. It is the same with the tongue and sweetmeats. The faculty of taste which resides in the tongue and the sweetness it perceives are both invisible. Thus also I give My children life and joy by means of the hidden manna,

which the world with all its wisdom knows not nor can know (Rev. ii. 7).

5. Sometimes during sickness the faculty of taste in the tongue is interfered with, and during that time, however tasty the food given to the sick person may be, it has an ill taste to him. In just the same way sin interferes with the taste for spiritual things. Under such circumstances My Word and service and My presence lose their attraction to the sinner, and instead of profiting by them he begins to argue about and to criticize them.

6. Many believers again--like the man born blind, on receiving his sight--are able to see Jesus as a prophet and the Son of Man, but do not regard Him as the Christ and the Son of God (John ix. 17, 35-37), until I am revealed to them a second time in power.

7. A mother once hid herself in a garden amongst some densely growing shrubs, and her little son went in search of her here and there, crying as he went. Through the whole garden he went, but could not find her. A servant said to him, "Sonny, don't cry! Look at the mangoes on this tree and all the pretty, pretty flowers in the garden. Come, I am going to get some for you." But the child cried out, "No! No! I want my mother. The food she gives me is nicer than all the mangoes, and her love is sweeter far than all these flowers, and indeed you know that all this garden is mine, for all that my mother has is mine. No! I want my mother!" When the mother, hidden in the bushes, heard this, she rushed out and, snatching her child to her breast, smothered him with kisses, and that garden became a paradise to the child. In this way My children cannot find in this great garden of a world, so

full of charming and beautiful things, any true joy until they find Me. I am their Emmanuel, who is ever with them, and I make Myself known to them (John xiv. 21).

8. Just as the sponge lies in the water, and the water fills the sponge, but the water is not the sponge and the sponge is not the water, but they ever remain different things, so children abide in Me and I in them. This is not pantheism, but it is the kingdom of God, which is set up in the hearts of those who abide in this world; and just as the water in the sponge, I am in every place and in everything, but they are not I (Luke xvii. 21).

9. Take a piece of charcoal, and however much you may wash it its blackness will not disappear, but let the fire enter into it and its dark colour vanishes. So also when the sinner receives the Holy Spirit (who is from the Father and Myself, for the Father and I are one), which is the baptism of fire, all the blackness of sin is driven away, and he is made a light to the world (Matt. iii. 11, 14). As the fire in the charcoal, so I abide in My children and they in Me, and through them I make Myself manifest to the world.

SECTION II

The Disciple,--
Master, if Thou wouldst make a special manifestation of Thyself to the world, men would no longer doubt the existence of God and Thy own divinity, but all would believe and enter on the path of righteousness.

The Master,--

1. My son, the inner state of every man I know well, and to each heart in accordance with its needs I make Myself known; and for bringing men into the way of righteousness there is no better means than the manifestation of Myself. For man I became man that he might know God, not as someone terrible and foreign, but as full of love and like to himself, for he is like Him and made in His image.

Man also has a natural desire that he should see Him in whom he believes and who loves him. But the Father cannot be seen, for He is by nature incomprehensible, and he who would comprehend Him must have the same nature. But man is a comprehensible creature, and being so cannot see God. Since, however, God is Love and He has given to man that same faculty of love, therefore, in order that that craving for love might be satisfied, He adopted a form of existence that man could comprehend. Thus He became man, and His children with all the holy angels may see Him and enjoy Him (Col. i. 15, ii. 9). Therefore I said that he that hath seen Me hath seen the Father (John xiv. 9-10). And although while in the form of man I am called the Son, I am the eternal and everlasting Father (Isa. ix. 6).

2. I and the Father and the Holy Spirit are One. Just as in the sun there are both heat and light, but the light is not heat, and the heat is not light, but both are one, though in their manifestation they have different forms, so I and the Holy Spirit, proceeding from the Father, bring light and heat to the world. The Spirit, which is the baptismal fire, burns to ashes in the hearts of believers all manner of sin and iniquity, making them pure and holy. I who am the True Light (John i. 9, viii. 12), dissipate all dark and evil desires, and leading them in the way of righteousness bring them at last to their

eternal home. Yet We are not three but One, just as the sun is but one.

3. Whatever worth and power and high faculty God has endowed man with must be brought into action, otherwise they gradually decay and die. In this way faith, if it is not truly fixed on the living God, is shattered by the shock of sin and transformed into doubt. Often one hears something like this, "If this or that doubt of mine be removed I am ready to believe." That is as though one with a broken limb should ask the doctor to take away the pain before he sets the limb. Surely this is folly, for the pain comes from the breaking of the limb, and when that is set the pain will of itself pass away. Thus by the act of sin man's tie with God has been snapped, and doubts, which are spiritual pains, have arisen. It needs must, therefore, that the union with God be again renewed, then those doubts which have arisen regarding My divinity and the existence of God will of themselves disappear. Then in place of pain there will come that wonderful peace which the world cannot give nor take away. Thus it was that I became flesh, that between God and poor broken men there might be union, and they might be happy with Him in heaven for evermore.

4. God is love, and in every living creature He has set this faculty of love, but especially in man. It is therefore nothing but right that the Lover who has given us life and reason and love itself should receive His due tribute of love. His desire is to all He has created, and if this love be not rightly used, and if we do not with all our heart and soul and mind and strength love Him who has endowed us with love, then that love falls from its high estate and becomes selfishness. Thus arises disaster both for ourselves and for other creatures of

God. Every selfish man, strangely enough, becomes a self-slayer.

This also I have said, "Love thy neighbour as thyself." Now although in a sense all men are neighbours one of another, yet the reference is especially to those who habitually live near each other, for it is an easy matter to live at peace with one who is near at hand for a few days only, even though he be unfriendly; but in the case of one who has his dwelling near you, and day by day is the cause of trouble to you, it is most difficult to bear with him, and love him as yourself. But when you have conquered in this great struggle it will be more easy to love all others as yourself.

When man with all his heart, mind, and soul loves God, and his neighbour as himself there will be no room for doubts, but in him will be established that Kingdom of God of which there should be no end, and he, melted and moulded in the fire of love, will be made into the image of his heavenly Father, who at the first made him like Himself.

5. Also I manifest Myself by means of My Word (the Bible) to those who seek Me with a sincere heart. Just as for the salvation of men I took on a human body, so My Word also, which is Spirit and Life (John vi.63) is written in the language of men, that is, there are inspired and human elements united in it. But just as men do not understand Me, so they do not understand My Word. To understand it a knowledge of the Hebrew and Greek tongues is not a necessity, but what is necessary is the fellowship of that Holy Spirit, abiding in whom the prophets and apostles wrote it. Without doubt the language of this Word is spiritual, and he who is born of the Spirit is alone able fully to understand it, whether he be

acquainted with the criticism of the world or be only a child, for that spiritual language is well understood by him since it is his mother tongue. But remember that those whose wisdom is only of this world cannot understand it, for they have no share in the Holy Spirit.

6. In the book of nature, of which I also am the Author, I freely manifest Myself. But for the reading of this book also spiritual insight is needed, that men may find Me, otherwise there is a danger lest instead of finding Me they go astray.

Thus the blind man uses the tips of his fingers as eyes, and by means of touch alone reads a book, but by touch alone can form no real estimate of its truth. The investigations of agnostics and skeptics prove this, for in place of perfection they see only defects. Fault finding critics ask, "If there is an Almighty Creator of the world why are there defects in it, such as hurricanes, earthquakes, eclipses, pain, suffering, death, and the like?" The folly of this criticism is similar to that of an unlearned man who finds fault with an unfinished building or an incomplete picture. After a time, when he sees them fully finished, he is ashamed of his folly, and ends by singing their praises. Thus too, God did not in one day give to this world its present form, nor will it in one day reach perfection. The whole creation moves onward to perfection, and if it were possible for the man of this world to see from afar with the eyes of God the perfect world in which no defect appears, he too would bow in praise before Him and say, "All is very good" (Gen. i.31).

7. The human spirit abides in the body very much as the chicken in the shell. If it were possible for the bird within the shell to be told that outside of it was a great widespread

world, with all kinds of fruit and flowers, with rivers and grand mountains, that its mother also was there, and that it would see all this when set free from its shell, it could not understand or believe it. Even if anyone told it that its feathers and eyes, ready now for use, would enable it to see and to fly, it would not believe it, nor would any proof be possible till it came out of its shell.

In the same way there are many who are uncertain about the future life and the existence of God, because they cannot see beyond this shell-like body of flesh, and their thoughts, like delicate wings, cannot carry them beyond the narrow confines of the brain. Their weak eyes cannot discover those eternal and unfading treasures which God has prepared for those who love Him (Isa. lxiv. 4, lxv. 17). The necessary condition for attaining to this eternal life is this, that while still in this body we should receive from the Holy Spirit by faith that life-giving warmth which the chicken receives from its mother, otherwise there is danger of death and eternal loss.

8. Again, many say that the thing, or the life, that has a beginning must of necessity have an end. This is not true, for is not the Almighty who is able at His will to make from naught a thing which is, also able by the word of His power to confer immortality on that which He has made? If not He cannot be called Almighty. Life in this world appears to be liable to decay and destruction, because it is in subjection to those things which are themselves the subject of change and decay. But if this life were set free from these changeful and decaying influences, and brought under the care of the eternal and unchanging God, who is the fountain and source of eternal life, it would escape from the clutch of death and attain to eternity.

As for those who believe on Me, "I give unto them eternal life, and they shall never perish, neither shall any man pluck them out of My hand" (John x. 28). "I am the Lord God Almighty that is and was and is to come" (Rev. i. 8).

II.

SIN AND SALVATION

The Disciple,--

Master, it is clear to almost everyone that to disobey God and to cease to worship Him is sin, and the deadly result is seen in the present state of the world. But what sin really is is not absolutely clear. In the very presence of Almighty God, and in opposition to His will, and in His own world, how did sin come to be?

The Master,--

1. Sin is to cast aside the will of God and to live according to one's own will, deserting that which is true and lawful in order to satisfy one's own desires, thinking thus to obtain happiness. Yet in so doing one does not obtain real happiness or enjoy true pleasure. Sin has no individuality, so that no one can say of it that someone created it. It is simply the name of a state or condition. There is only one Creator and He is good, and a good Creator could not have created a bad thing, for to do so would be against His very nature. And apart from the one Creator there is no other who could have created sin. Satan can only spoil that which has already been created, but he has not the power of creating anything. So sin is not a part of creation, nor has it independent existence such that it could be created. It is simply a delusive and destructive state of being.

For instance, light is something which has real existence, but darkness has not; it is only a state, the absence of light. Thus sin or evil is not a self-existent thing, but simply the absence or nonexistence of good. This dark state of evil is most terrible, for because of it many miss the right course, and making shipwreck on the rocks of Satan fall into the darkness of hell and are lost. For this reason I who am the Light of the world became manifest in the flesh, so that those who put their trust in Me should not perish, for I rescue them from the power of darkness and bring them safe to that desired and heavenly haven, where there is neither name nor sign of darkness (Rev. xxi. 23, xxii. 5).

2. You ask how this dark state of sin came to be in the very presence of the Lord of creation. It arose because Satan and men, of their own motion in an unlawful and wrong way, sought to carry out their own desires. And if you ask why God did not make man in such a way that he could not fall into such a state, the answer is that if he had been constructed like a machine he could never have attained to that state of happiness which is reached only by action in accordance with one's own choice. Adam and Eve fell into the wiles and deceit of Satan because in their sinless state they did not know there were such things as lies and deceit. Before this, Satan himself did not know of the existence of that pride by reason of which he was cast out of heaven, for before him no such thing as pride existed. And although both in men and Satan this state of sin came to be, God by His almighty power has given that state a new aspect, so that even from it He has brought forth the noblest results.

First of all, the boundless love of God was made manifest in the incarnation and redemption, which under other circumstances would have remained hidden; and in the second place, the redeemed, after having tasted the bitterness of sin, will more richly enjoy the happiness of heaven, just as after a taste of bitterness the sweetness of honey gives greater delight. For in heaven they sin no more, but in meekness and obedient love they serve their Father God, and abide with Him in joy for evermore.

3. Men are keen on discovering faults in the sun and moon, such as spots and eclipses, but to the spots and eclipses of sin they give no heed. From this you may measure how great that darkness in men is, when the very light they have is darkness (Matt. vi.23). Just as the body of the leper by reason of his disease becomes numb and insensible, so the heart and mind of man by reason of sin become dull and insensate, and bring to him no sense of disgust or pain. But the time will come when he will awake to its terrible ravages, and then there will be weeping and gnashing of teeth.

4. Many who are immersed in sin are unaware of its load, just as one who dives into the water may have tons of water upon him, but is wholly unaware of its weight until he is choked in death. But he who emerges from the water and seeks to carry some away soon finds its weight, however little he takes up; and he who, finding the burden of his sin, comes to Me in penitence will freely receive true rest, for it is such I come to seek and to save (Matt. xi.28, Luke xix.10).

5. It is not necessary that every single member of the body should become useless and weak before death occurs. A weakness of, or a blow upon, the heart or the brain will

suffice to bring an end to life, however strong and healthy other parts of the body may be. Thus one sin by its poisonous effect on the mind and heart is sufficient to ruin the spiritual life not of one only, but of a whole family or nation, even of the whole race. Such was the sin of Adam. But as one word from Me could bring Lazarus from the tomb, even so it is sufficient to give eternal life to all.

6. Sometimes it happens that an animal or bird after long association with man returns to its own kind, but they, instead of welcoming it, set upon it and do it to death, the reason being that by its long residence and familiarity with man, its habits and manner of life have entirely changed. In the same way as animals do not admit to their society those of their kind that have come under man's influence, how can the saint and angels in heaven welcome those sinners who have lived in intimate relations with wicked men? This does not mean that saints and angels have no love for sinful men, but the holy atmosphere of heaven will itself be distasteful to such men. For clearly, when in this world sinners dislike the company of good men, how can they be happy in their company throughout eternity? To them a heaven of that sort would be as distasteful as hell itself. Do not suppose that God or His people will turn sinners out of heaven and cast them into hell, for God who is Love, never cast anyone into hell, nor ever will do so. It is the foul life of the sinner that will bring him to hell. Long before the end of life brings heaven and hell near to us, there has been set up in every man's heart, according to his good or evil nature, his own heaven or hell. Therefore whosoever longs to be saved from that eternal torment, let him truly repent of his sins and give his heart to Me, that by My presence with him and the Holy Spirit's

influence, he may become forever a child of the kingdom of God.

7. A rebel against a king or government in this world may save himself by taking refuge in another country, but where shall a rebel against God flee for safety? Wherever he goes, even in heaven or hell, he will find God ever present. (Psa. cxxxix.7,8). He will find his safety only in repentance and submission to his Lord.

8. For Adam and Eve the fig leaves were too scanty a covering, so God gave them coats of skin. In this way, too, man's good deeds are as useless as the fig leaves to save him from the wrath to come. Nothing will suffice save My robe of righteousness.

9. The moth thinks not of the burning and destructive power of the flame, but fascinated by its brilliancy rushes into it and perishes. So man, regardless of the destructive and poisonous power of sin, and feeling only its allurement, rushes in to his eternal destruction. But My light rescues the sinner from death, and bestows upon him life and enduring happiness. Man was so made as to be capable of appropriating the precious gift of My true light.

10. Sin is not an illusion or a thing of the imagination, but in this state of spiritual darkness, by the exercise of the evil will of man,such living seeds of evil have come into existence as will for ever infect his spirit and finally destroy it--just as smallpox in quite a short time will destroy the beauty of a man for all time, turning it to repulsive ugliness. As God did not create wickedness, so also He did not create disease and bodily pains. They are simply the natural issue of man's

disobedience. Pain and disease also are not things of the imagination, but are the outward and visible fruits of the hidden unseen disease of sin, whether it be one's own sin or that of the family of which one is a member. When all these members repent and are united with Me, My health-giving blood circulates through all, healing all their internal and unseen diseases and giving to them health for all eternity. For such a state of health man was created, that he might for ever dwell in happiness with his Lord and Master.

SECTION II

The Disciple,--
Master, in these days some learned men and their followers regard Thy atonement and the redemption by blood as meaningless and futile, and say that Christ was only a great teacher and example for our spiritual life, and that salvation and eternal happiness depend on our own efforts and good deeds.

The Master,--
1. Never forget that spiritual and religious ideas are connected less with the head than with the heart, which is the temple of God, and when the heart is filled with the presence of God the head also is enlightened. For the mind and the eyes of the understanding are useless without the true light, as the natural eyes are without daylight. In the dark one may mistake a rope for a snake, just as the wise of this world pervert spiritual truth and lead astray simple minds. So Satan when beguiling Eve made use not of the sheep or the dove but of the serpent, the most crafty of all the animals. So he takes the wisdom of the wise and the skill of the learned, and of them makes

instruments suited to his purpose. But it is not enough to be learned and clever; one must also have the innocence of the dove, therefore I have said, "Be ye wise as serpents and harmless as doves" (Matt. x.16).

2. My cross and atonement do the same for believers as the serpent of brass did for the Israelites, for whoever looked up to that with the eyes of faith was saved (Num. xxi.9, John iii.14,15). There were some, however, who, instead of believing, thought of it as brass only and began to criticize and say, "If Moses had provided an antidote, or were to give us some powerful drug or special medicine for these venomous serpents, that would be a proper object of faith, but what power has this pole over poisonous venom?" They all died. In these days too, those who cavil about the method of salvation which God has appointed will perish in the poison of their own sin.

3. A young man fell down a precipice and was so much injured, and lost so much blood that he was at the point of death. When his father took him to the doctor he said, "The life is the blood, and the supply of this young man's blood is exhausted; but if anyone is prepared to sacrifice his own life he may recover, otherwise he will die." The father, whose heart was overflowing with love for his son, offered his own blood, and this being injected into the young man's veins he recovered. Man has fallen from the mount of holiness and lies broken and wounded by his sins, and by reason of those wounds his spiritual life has ebbed away and he is near to death. But for those who believe in Me I pour forth my own everlasting and spiritual blood, that they may be saved from death and obtain eternal life. For this purpose have I come

that they might have life and have it more abundantly (John x.10), and thus live for evermore.

4. In ancient times men were forbidden to drink the blood of animals, or to eat certain foods, in the belief that they would thus escape certain diseases; and also lest, as a man has an animal body, his animal propensities might be strengthened by eating flesh and drinking blood. But now "My flesh is meat indeed and My blood is drink indeed" (John vi.55), for they give spiritual life, and by them perfect health and heavenly happiness and joy are received.

5. The forgiveness of sins does not mean full salvation, for that can only come with perfect freedom from sin. For it is possible that a man should die from the disease of his sin, though he has received full pardon for it. For instance, a man had his brain affected owing to an illness of long standing, and whilst thus affected he made an attack upon another man and killed him. When sentence of death was pronounced upon him, his relatives explained the circumstances and appealed for mercy for him, and he was granted pardon for the sin of murder. But before his friends could reach him with the good news, indeed while they were on the way, he had died of the sickness by reason of which he had committed the murder. What advantage was this pardon to the murderer? His real safety would have been to be cured of his disease, and then he would have had real happiness in his pardon. For this reason I became manifest in the flesh that I might deliver penitent believers from the disease of sin, from its punishment and from death; thus taking away both cause and effect. They will not die in their sins, for I will save them (Matt. i.21), and they shall pass from death to becomes heirs of eternal life.

6. To many people life is full of peril, and they are like that hunter who caught sight of a honeycomb on the branch of a tree overhanging a stream. Climbing up, he began to enjoy the honey, quite unaware of the fact that he was in peril of death, for in the stream beneath him lay an alligator with open jaws waiting to devour him, while around the foot of the tree a pack of wolves had gathered waiting for him to descend. Worse still, the tree on which he sat had been eaten away at the roots by an insect and it was ready to fall. In a short time it did fall, and the unwary hunter became the prey of the alligator. Thus, too, the human spirit, ensconced in the body, enjoys for a short time the false and fleeting pleasures of sin gathered in the honeycomb of the brain, without a thought that it is in the midst of this fearsome jungle of the world. There Satan sits ready to tear it to pieces, and hell like an alligator waits with open mouth to gulp it down, while, worst of all, the tiny unseen insect of sin has eaten away the very roots of the body and life. Soon the soul falls and becomes an everlasting prey to hell. But the sinner who comes to Me I will deliver from sin, from Satan, and from hell, and will give him eternal joy "which none shall take away from him" (John xvi.22).

7. Satan with crafty speech and enticements draws men to him and swallows them down just as a snake fascinates little birds by the magnetism of its glittering eye, and makes a prey of them. But to those who believe on Me I give deliverance from that old serpent and from the seductions of this soul-destroying world. I set them free so that, as a bird, easily resisting the force of gravity which is in the earth, flies freely through the open heaven, they mount on the wings of prayer

and reach at last the abode of safety and their hearts dear home, drawn by the sweet attractions of My love.

8. Just as a man with jaundice sees everything yellow, so to the sinner and the philosopher truth itself takes on the form and fashion of his sin or his theories, and it is not a matter of much surprise if such people go a step further and count Me a sinner like themselves. But My work, which is the salvation of sinners, does not depend on the good opinion of the world, but for ever moves on its undisturbed way in the lives of believers. Just as Levi, being still in the loins of Abraham, paid tithe to Me though he was not yet born, so all generations of believers have in Me, offered upon the cross, the atonement and ransom for their sins, though they were not at that time even born; for this salvation is for all races of men in the world.

9. This saying, that a man can by his own effort and good works acquire salvation, is foolish and absurd so long as the man is not born again. World-rulers and teachers of morality say, "Become good by doing good," but this is what I say, "Become good yourself before doing good works." When that new and good life has been entered upon, good deeds will be the natural result.

It is only a fool that will say that a bitter tree by constantly bearing fruit will at last become sweet. As a matter of fact a bitter tree can become sweet by being grafted on a sweet tree, so that the life and qualities peculiar to the sweet tree will pass into the bitter one and its natural bitterness will pass away. This is what we call a new creation. So too the sinner may have the desire to do what is right, and yet the only result is sin; but when he repents and by faith is grafted into Me the old man in him dies, and he becomes a new creature. Then from this new life which has its origin in salvation good deeds come forth as fruit, and this fruit abides for ever.

10. There are many who have learnt from experience that man's natural goodness cannot give true peace of heart, nor can it give him a certainty of salvation or eternal life. The young man who came to Me seeking eternal life is a case in point. His first thought with regard to Me was wrong, as is that of some worldly-wise men and their followers at the present day. He thought Me to be one of those teachers who are like whited sepulchres, and in whose lives there is not a particle of true goodness. Therefore I said to him, "Why do you ask Me about goodness? There is none good but One." But he failed to see in Me the one giver of goodness and life; and when I sought to admit him to My companionship and make him a truly good man, and bestow life upon him, he became sad and left Me. His life, however, makes one thing perfectly clear, and that is that his keeping the commandments and his goodness did not satisfy him or give him the assurance of eternal life. If his good works had given him peace he would not have come to inquire of Me, or had he come he would not have left Me in sorrow, but, believing My words, would have gone away rejoicing.

Not long afterwards the young man Paul recognized Me, and the desire of his heart was completely fulfilled. Instead of turning away in sadness he gave up all that he had and followed Me (Phil. iii.6-15). So everyone who ceases to trust in his own righteousness and follows Me shall receive from Me true peace and everlasting life.

III.
PRAYER

The Disciple,--
Sometimes this question is asked, "Since God is fully aware of our needs, and knows how to supply them in the best way, not for the good only but for the evil, how should we pray to Him about them? Whether our necessities be temporal or spiritual, can we by our prayers alter the will of God?"

The Master,--
1. Those who ask such a question show clearly that they do not know what prayer is. They have not lived a prayerful life, or they would know that prayer to God is not a form of begging. Prayer does not consist in an effort to obtain from God the things which are necessary for this life. Prayer is an effort to lay hold of God Himself, the Author of life, and when we have found Him who is the source of life and have entered into communion with Him, then the whole of life is ours and with Him all that will make life is perfect. To evildoers, God, out of love for them, gives what is necessary for their life in this world, but their spiritual necessities He does not even show to them, as they have no spiritual life. Were He to bestow such spiritual blessings upon them, they would not be able to appreciate them. But on those who believe gifts of both kinds are bestowed, especially spiritual blessings, with the result that very soon they pay little regard

to temporal blessings, but fix their love on the unseen and spiritual. We cannot alter the will of God, but the man of prayer can discover the will of God with regard to himself. For to men of this kind God makes Himself manifest in the hidden chamber of the heart, and holds communion with them; and when His gracious purposes are shown to be for their good, then the doubts and difficulties of which they complain pass away for ever.

2. Prayer is, as it were, a breathing in of the Holy Spirit, and God so pours His Holy Spirit into the life of the prayerful that they become "living souls" (Gen. ii.7; John xx.22). They will never die, for the Holy Spirit pours Himself by means of prayer into their spiritual lungs, and fills their spirits with health and vigour and everlasting life.

God, who is Love, has freely bestowed on all men those things which are necessary for both the spiritual and temporal life, but since He offers salvation and His Holy Spirit to all as freely, they are lightly esteemed. But prayer teaches us to value them, because they are as necessary as air and water, heat and light, without which life is impossible. The things for our spiritual life God has freely provided, but men so lightly regard them that they offer no thanks to their Creator; but on the other hand, His gifts of gold, silver, and precious jewels, which are scarce and obtained with great difficulty, they highly esteem, though with such things the hunger and thirst of the body cannot be assuaged, nor the longings of the heart be satisfied. With such folly do men of the world act with regard to spiritual things, but to the man of prayer are given true wisdom and eternal life.

3. This world is like a widespread ocean in which men sink and are drowned, but marine animals carry on their life in the deepest water, because they occasionally come to the surface and, opening their mouths, take in a certain amount of air, which enables them to live in the depths. So they who rise to the surface of this life-ocean, by means of private prayer breathe in the life-giving Spirit of God, and find even in this world life and safety.

4. Although fish spend their whole life in the salt water of the sea, yet they do not themselves become salty, because they have life in them; so the man of prayer, though he has to live in this sin-defiled world, remains free of the sinful taint, because by means of prayer his life is maintained.

5. Just as the salt water of the sea is drawn upwards by the hot rays of the sun, and gradually takes on the form of clouds, and, turned thus into sweet and refreshing water, falls in showers on the earth (for the sea water as it rises upwards leaves behind it its salt and bitterness), so when the thoughts and desires of the man of prayer rise aloft like misty emanations of the soul, the rays of the Sun of Righteousness purify them of all sinful taint, and his prayers become a great cloud which descends from heaven in a shower of blessing, bringing refreshment to many on the earth.

6. Just as the waterfowl spends its life swimming in the water, yet when in flight its feathers are perfectly dry, so men of prayer have their abode in this world, but when the time comes for them to fly aloft they pass from this sin-polluted world and arrive without spot or stain at their everlasting home of rest.

7. The ship, quite properly, has its place in the water, but for the water to flow into the ship is both unsuitable and dangerous. So for a man to have his abode in this world is right and good for himself and others, for, keeping himself afloat, he will be able to help them to arrive along with himself at the haven of life. But for the world to find its way into his heart means death and destruction. Therefore the man of prayer ever reserves his heart for Him who formed it to be His temple, and thus both in this world and that which is to come he rests in peace and safety.

8. We all know that without water it is impossible to live; but if we sink beneath it we choke and die. While we need to make use of and drink water, we ought not to fall into and sink beneath it. Therefore the world and worldly things must be used with discretion, for without them life is not only difficult but impossible. For this very purpose God created the world that men might make use of it, but men should not drown themselves in it, for thus the breath of prayer is stopped and they perish.

9. If by ceasing to live the life of prayer the life of the spirit begins to fail, then those worldly things which are intended to be useful become hurtful and destructive. The sun by its light and heat makes all vegetable things to live and flourish, and also causes them to wither and die. The air also gives life and vigour to all living beings, but itself is the cause of their decomposition. Therefore "Watch and Pray."

10. We ought so to live in this world that though we are in it we are not of it, and then the things of this world instead of being hurtful will be useful, and will help the growth of the spiritual life; but only on this condition, that the spirit ever

keeps its face turned towards the Sun of Righteousness. Thus it sometimes happens that in a plot of unclean and filthy ground flowers spring up and flourish, and the sweet scent of the flowers overpowers the evil smell of the place. The plants, turning towards the sun, receive from it light and heat, and the filth instead of being hurtful to the plants fertilizes them and helps them to grow and flourish. So, too, the man of prayer as he prays turns his heart to Me, and receives from Me light and warmth, and amidst the ill odours of this evil world the sweet scent of his new and holy life glorifies Me, and there is produced in him not sweet odours only, but also fruit which shall abide for ever.

SECTION II

1. To pray does not imply that without prayer God would not give us anything or that He would be unaware of our needs, but it has this great advantage, that in the attitude of prayer the soul is best fitted to receive the Giver of blessing as well as those blessings He desires to bestow. Thus it was that the fullness of the Spirit was not poured out upon the Apostles on the first day, but after ten days of special preparation.

If a blessing were conferred upon one without a special readiness for it, he would neither value it sufficiently nor long retain it. For instance, because Saul obtained the Holy Spirit and the kingship without seeking for them he very soon lost them both, for he had set out from home not to obtain the Holy Spirit but to look for his lost asses (1 Sam. ix.3; x. 11; v. 13-14; xxxi.4).

2. The man of prayer alone can worship God in spirit and truth. Others are like the sensitive plant; during worship, affected by the teaching and presence of the Holy Spirit, they shrivel up, as it were, and bowing their heads become serious, but scarcely have they left the church before they brighten up and go on as before.

3. If we do not take care of a tree or a shrub which bears good fruit or flowers, it will degenerate and go back to its wild state. In the same way, if the believer, through the neglect of prayer and the spiritual life, ceases to abide in Me, he will, because of this carelessness, fall from that state of blessedness, and sinking again into his old sinful ways be lost.

4. When we see a crane standing motionless on the side of a tank or lake, we may suppose from his attitude that he is musing on the glory of God or the excellent quality of the water. But no such thing! He stand there motionless for hours, but the moment he catches sight of a frog or small fish he springs upon it and gulps it down. Just such is the attitude and method of many with regard to prayer and religious meditation. Seated by the shore of the boundless ocean of God, they give no thought to His majesty and love, or to His divine nature that cleanses from sin and satisfies the hungry soul, but are wrapped up in the thought of acquiring some specially desired object, by means of which they may more fully indulge in the delights of this fleeting world. Thus they turn away from the fountain of true peace, and, immersing themselves in the fading joys of this world, with them also die and pass away.

5. Water and petrol both come from the earth, and though they seem to be alike and even the same, they are in nature

and purpose exact opposites, for the one extinguishes fire and the other adds fuel to it. So also the world and its treasures, the heart and its thirst for God are alike His creation. Now the result of the attempt to satisfy the heart with the wealth and pride and honours of this world is the same as if one tried to put out a fire with petrol, for the heart can only find ease and satisfaction in Him who created both it and the longing desire of which it is conscious (Ps. xlii.1,2). Therefore whoever now comes to Me I will give to him that living water so that he will never again thirst, but it shall be in him a well of water springing up into eternal life (John iv.14).

6. Men try in vain to find peace in the world and the things of the world, for experience plainly shows that true peace and satisfaction are not to be found in them. They are like the boy who found an onion and began peeling off its skins in the hope of finding something inside it, just as one finds in a box on taking the lid off. But his was an altogether futile expectation, since he found nothing but the last skin, for an onion is nothing but a collection of skins. And this world and all that belongs to it has been proved to be vanity of vanities (Eccles. xii.8), until men discover the true fountain of peace (Isa. lv.1; Jer. ii.13; Rev. xxii.17).

7. The world is like a mirage, and the truth seeker, hoping to find something to satisfy his thirsty spirit, starts off in search of it but meets with nothing but disappointment and despair. The water of life cannot be found in man-made tanks or cracked cisterns; but those who approach Me in prayer with a pure heart will find in Me, who am the source of the living water, that from which they may obtain satisfaction, invigoration, and eternal life (Isa. lv.1; Jer. ii.13; Rev. xxii.17).

8. A woman was traveling along a mountain track, carrying her child in her arms, when the child, catching sight of a pretty flower, made such a spring out of its mother's arms that it fell headlong down the mountain side, struck its head upon a rock, and died on the spot. Now it is perfectly clear that the safety and sustenance of the child were to be found in its mother's bosom, and not in those fascinating flowers which were the cause of its death. So acts the believer whose life is not a life of prayer. When he catches sight of the fleeting and fascinating pleasures of the world he forgets My love and care which are far greater than those of the mother, and, neglecting that spiritual milk which I provide for him, leaps out of My arms and is lost.

9. The sustenance which the mother provides is so arranged that it cannot be obtained without some effort on the part of the infant. So also My children whom I bear in My bosom cannot obtain without seeking, the spiritual milk which is able to save their souls. And as the child does not need to be taught, but knows by instinct where and how to obtain its food, so those who are born of the Spirit know by a spiritual instinct, and not from worldly philosophy or wisdom, how to pray and to obtain from Me, their spiritual Mother, the milk of eternal life.

10. I have infused into man's nature hunger and thirst, that he may not in sheer heedlessness regard himself as God, but that day by day he may be reminded of his needs and that his life is bound up with the life and existence of Someone who created him. Thus being made aware of his defects and necessities, he may abide in Me and I in him, and then he will ever find in Me his happiness and joy.

SECTION III

1. To pray is as it were to be on speaking terms with Me, and so by being in communion with and abiding in Me to become like Me. There is a kind of insect which feeds upon and lives among grass and green leaves and becomes like them in colour. Also the polar bear dwelling among the white snows has the same snowy whiteness, and the tiger of Bengal bears upon its skin the marks of the reeds among which it lives. So those, who by means of prayer abide in communion with Me partake, with the saints and angels, of My Nature, and being formed in My image become like Me.

2. When for but a short time I drew Peter, James, and John into communion with Me upon the Mount, I showed them somewhat of My glory, and of all the saints two only, Moses and Elias, appeared to them; they were so captivated with that brief glimpse of heavenly glory that they wished to erect three tabernacles in order to live there (Matt. xvii.1-5). How wonderful, then, will be the happiness of those who abide in Me, and with saints and angels innumerable enter into their longed-for heaven, and share with Me My full glory which knows no loss nor shadow of change (John xvii.24; James i.17). The man of prayer shall never be alone, but he shall abide with Me and My holy ones forever (Matt. xxviii.20; Zach. iii.7-8).

3. It is not a great thing to control and make use of wild animals, lightning, the wind, and light, and other powers of nature, but to gain the mastery over the world and Satan and self, with all its passions, is of a truth a most momentous and necessary thing. Upon those only who live a life of prayer do I bestow the power to overcome all the might of the enemy

(Luke x.17,20), so that even while they live in this world they abide with Me in the heavenly places (Eph. ii.6), and Satan being below and they above he is never able to reach them, but they abide forever with Me in safety and without a tremor of fear.

Although men have now obtained control over the powers of nature they are not to travel beyond the bounds of the air, while the man of prayer, having mastered Satan and self, can range at will the everlasting heavens.

4. Just as the bee collects the sweet juice of the flowers and turns it into honey without injuring their colour or fragrance, so the man of prayer gathers happiness and profit from all God's creation without doing any violence to it. As bees also gather their honey from flowers in all sorts of different places and store it in the honeycomb, so the man of God gathers sweet thoughts and feelings from every part of creation, and in communion with his Creator collects in his heart the honey of truth, and in enduring peace with Him at all times and in all places, tastes with delight the sweet honey of God.

5. Now is the time to obtain and keep in the vessels of our hearts the oil of the Holy Spirit, as the five wise virgins did (Matt. xxv.1-13); otherwise like the five foolish ones we shall meet with nothing but grief and despair. Now also you must collect the manna for the true Sabbath, otherwise there will be nothing left you but sorrow and woe (Ex. xvi.15,27). "Pray, therefore, that your flight may not be in the winter," that is, in time of great distress or the last days, "or on the Sabbath day," that is, the reign of a thousand years of eternal rest, for such an opportunity will never occur again (Matt. xxiv.20).

In the same way as climate produces a change in form, colour, and the habits of growth in plants and flowers, so those who maintain communion with Me undergo a development of their spiritual nature in habit, appearance, and disposition; and putting off the old man they are transformed into My own glorious and incorruptible image.

6. With my finger I wrote upon the ground the sinful state of each of those who, regardless of their inner vileness, brought the woman taken in adultery for condemnation, so that they left her one by one and went away abashed and ashamed. With My finger, too, I point out in secret to My servants their wounds of sin, and when they repent, with a touch of the same finger I heal them; and in the same way as a child grasps his father's finger and by it help walks along with him, so I with My finger lead My children along the road from this world to their home of rest and everlasting peace (John xiv.2,3).

7. Oftentimes men pray to the Father in My name, but do not abide in Me, that is, they take My name into their mouths and on their lips, but not into their hearts and lives. That is the reason why they do not obtain what they pray for. But when I abide in them and they in Me, then whatever they ask from the Father they receive, because they pray under the direction of the Holy Spirit in that condition. The Holy Spirit shows them what will glorify the Father and be best for themselves and for others. Otherwise they will get such an answer as a bad son got from a governor whom his father had served with great courage and honour. When the son presented a petition in his father's name and asked for some employment and favour, the governor pointed out to him his

evil life and habits, and said, "Do not petition me in your father's name, but first go and act according to his example. Let his high worth be not on your lips only, but carry it into your life, and then your petition will be accepted."

8. Between the prayers of those who worship and praise Me with their lips only and of those who do so from their heart there is a very great difference. For instance, one who was a true worshipper was constantly praying for another that his eyes might be opened and that he might accept the truth, while the other was a worshipper in name only often prayed in his enmity against My true worshipper that he might be struck blind. Finally the prayers of the true worshipper were heard by the loving will of God, and he who was formerly only a hypocrite received spiritual sight. With his heart full of joy this man became a true believer, and a sincere and lasting brother of My true servant.

9. Prayer makes things possible for men which they find impossible by other means, and they experience such wonderful things in life as are not only opposed to the rules and opinions of worldly wisdom, but are held to be impossible altogether. Scientific men do not recognize that He who set all created things in order and made laws for them, cannot be imprisoned behind the bars of his own laws. The ways of the great Lawgiver are inscrutable, because His eternal will and purpose is the blessing and prosperity of all His creatures, and the reason the natural man cannot grasp this fact is because spiritual things are spiritually discerned (1 Cor. ii.14).

The greatest of all miracles is the new birth in man, and to the man who has experienced this miracle all others become possible. Now in very cold countries a bridge of water is a common sight, because when the surface of a river is frozen hard the water beneath still flows freely on, but men cross over the icy bridge with ease and safety. But if one were to speak of a bridge of water spanning a flowing river to people who are constantly perspiring in the heat of a tropical clime, they would at once say that such a thing was impossible and against the laws of nature. There is the same great difference between those who have been born again and by prayer maintain their spiritual life, and those who live worldly lives and value only material things, and so are utterly ignorant of the life of the soul.

10. He who desires by prayer to obtain from God the blessing of a spiritual life must believe and obey without questioning. The man who came to Me with a withered hand, when I commanded him to stretch out his hand instantly obeyed, and so his hand became whole as the other (Matt. xii.10-13). But suppose instead of that instant obedience he had begun to argue and say, "How can I stretch out my hand? If I had been able to do that, why should I have come to Thee? First of all heal my hand, and then I shall be able to stretch it out." All this would have been considered very reasonable and to the point, but his hand would never have been healed. He who prays must believe and be obedient, and stretch out to Me in prayer his weak and withered hands, and then it will be for Me to give him spiritual life, and according to his need it shall be granted to him (Matt. xxi.22).

IV.
SERVICE

The Disciple,--
Master, what is the real meaning of service? Is it that we serve the Creator and then His creatures for His sake? Is the help of man, who is after all but a mere worm, of any value to God in caring for His great family, or does God stand in need of the help of man in protecting or preserving any of His creatures?

The Master,--
1. Service means the activity of the spiritual life and is the natural offering prompted by love. God, who is Love, is ever active in the care of His creation, and His desire is that His creatures and especially man, whom He formed in His own image and likeness, should never be idle. In the care and preservation of His creatures God needs the help of none, for He created them in such a way that without His help they could not continue to exist, and He it is who has provided all that is required to satisfy their desires. In true service of others there is this great advantage that it helps him who serves— just as it happened to you in Tibet. When you were in fear of death on account of the bitter cold, you saw one lying buried in the snow and at the point of death, you went to him and lifting him on to your shoulders carried him forward, and the

efforts you made produced heat in your body which also passed into his, and both he and you were saved, so that in rescuing him you saved your own life. This is the true end of service. No one can live alone and deprived of the help of others. Should anyone receive help from another, and be unwilling to return such assistance as he can, such an ungrateful fellow would have no right to expect any help from any one at all.

2. Until a man brings into the service of God and man faculties and powers with which God has endowed him, he will not receive from God the help He alone can bestow. As soon as man does his part God will complete it. For instance, the removal of the stone from the grave of Lazarus was man's work, and it was not necessary for God to put forth His power to do that; but when the people had rolled away the stone, then God, that is Myself, did that which was beyond the power and skill of man, for I gave life to the dead. Even after that there was work for man to do in releasing Lazarus from the grave-clothes that he might be perfectly free (John xi.39,41,44).

So with regard to those who are dead in sin. It is the work of My disciples to roll away the gravestones of hindrance and difficulty, but to bestow life is My work. Often, too, some who have received spiritual life still remain in bondage to their old bad habits and evil associations, and it is the duty of My children to lead them into perfect freedom; and to render this great service they should ever be alert in heart and soul.

3. A certain king on his deathbed spoke to a faithful servant of his as follows: "It has been my custom when setting out on a journey to send you before me to announce me and make

preparations for my reception. I am going to the land of the dead. Go, therefore, and inform them that I am about to join them." At first the honest servant did not understand what his lord meant, but as soon as he saw that his meaning was that he should die and thus precede him to the land of the dead, the faithful fellow, without a moment's hesitation or doubt, plunged a sword into his heart, and thus entered the country of the dead, there to await his lord. Thus it is the duty of those who serve Me, who am the Lord of Life and the King of kings (Acts iii.15; Rev. xix.16), to carry the gospel of salvation to those who are dead in sin, and to be ready even to give their lives for Me, who came to earth for their salvation and will come yet once more (Rev. ii.10).

4. A rebellious son once left his father's house and joined a band of robbers and became in time as bold and ruthless as the rest. The father called his servants and ordered them to go to his son and tell him that if he would repent and return home all would be forgiven, and he would receive him into his home. But the servants, in dread of the wild country and fierce robbers, refused to go. Then the elder brother of the young man, who loved him as his father did, set off to carry the message of forgiveness. But soon after he had entered the jungle a band of robbers set upon him and mortally wounded him. The younger brother was one of the band, and when he recognized his elder brother he was filled with grief and remorse. The elder brother managed to give the message of forgiveness and then, saying that the purpose of his life was fulfilled and love's duty done, he gave up the ghost. This sacrifice of the elder brother made so deep an impression on the rebellious youth that he went back in penitence to his father and from that day forward lived a new life. Is it not right, therefore, that My sons should be prepared to sacrifice

their lives in order to bring the message of mercy to those of their brethren who have gone astray and are ruined in sin, just as I also gave My life for the salvation of all?

5. My children are like salt in the world (Matt. v.13). If the salt crystals are not dissolved they cannot transmit their flavour. So with My children. If they are not melted in the fire of love and the Holy Spirit, and made into a living sacrifice, they will not be able to bring a single soul that spiritual and heavenly life by which they may be saved. They will be no better than Lot's wife who became a pillar of salt (Gen. xix.26). But just as for your sakes I was melted in Gethesemane (Luke xxii.44), and on the cross gave up My life that I might save the lives of men, for life must be paid for with life, so you also are called upon to give up your lives and thus bring the savour of spiritual life to others and deliver them from death.

6. A certain murderer, instead of being hanged, was sent into battle, and there he fought for his king and country with such dauntless courage that although he was severely wounded he came back a conqueror. After the victory he was brought into the court again to be sentenced. The king, seeing on his body the marks of his wounds, cancelled the sentence of death, and not only forgave his crime, but also highly rewarded him and raised him to a post of honour. So those who on My side fight in the Holy War against Satan with courage and boldness that they may save their brethren and sisters, shall not only receive from Me the forgiveness of their sins, but in the kingdom of God I will bestow on them a crown and a kingdom (James v.20; Rev. iii.21).

7. As the pipe that is used to convey clean water is itself kept clean by the water which passes through it, so those, who through the Holy Spirit carry the Water of Life to others, are themselves purified and become heirs to the kingdom of God.

8. The best way for the believer to be fitted for the reception of the Holy Spirit and for service is to be obedient to the heavenly voice and immediately, as far as ability goes, to begin to serve. As to become a good swimmer it is useless to receive instruction unless one enters the water and strikes out for oneself, and only by constantly practising, first in shallow water and then in deep, can one become an adept in the art, so, in order to learn how to save the souls of those who are sinking in the dark waters of sin, the best way is to enter the only real and practical school of divinity, which is union with Myself (Acts iv.13).

9. There are some who are kept back from serving by the thought of their lack of ability, and do not remember that My strength gives power in weakness (2 Cor. xii.9). They are like invalids who, though they have recovered from their disease and are taking nourishing food, yet remain weak because they do no work and take no proper exercise. What such believers need is that they should put their trust in Me and set out to save sinners from destruction.

SECTION II

1. Love is the touchstone by which the reality of truth is perceived, and by it shall all men know that ye are My disciples (John xiii.35). I also make use of the sword of justice, so that at first sight some are inclined to think that, like Solomon, I intend to finish My work without mercy (1

Kings iii.16-28), but My object, like his, is to apply the touchstone of love which will bring out the truth, and show that you are the children of that God of Love who gave His life to save yours. You ought therefore to abide in that love and serve one another, and even give your lives to serve others, as I also gave My life for you. Then as I live ye shall live also (John xiv.19).

2. If ye are My disciples indeed your service of love will bear much fruit (John xv.8). And if men speak evil of you and pelt you with reproaches, pray for them, and instead of reproaching them let them taste the sweet fruit of your love.

Mischievous boys, when they catch sight of sweet fruit on a tree, pelt it with stones, and the tree without a murmur drops upon them, instead of stones, its charming fruit. For the tree has no stones to throw, but what God has given it, it gives without complaining. Be not cast down by ill treatment, for the fact that men fling abuse at you is full proof that yours is a fruitful life. Though they treat you thus from envy and spite, yet by that means the glory of your heavenly Father is made manifest. Do not suppose that God hungers after glory, or that there is anything lacking in His glory that man can supply. By no means! The object of His love is to lift that mean creature man out of the sinful state into which he has fallen and bear him upwards to His heaven of glory. Thus He gives not glory to Himself but to man by cleansing and purifying him, and in this the wonder and majesty of His love is made manifest.

3. To those who by their labours have enabled many to turn from sin and find righteousness in Me, I will grant such glory that they shall first of all shine like the stars, and then being

made perfect shall shine like the sun in the kingdom of their Father. The stars fade and disappear at the rising of the Sun of Righteousness, but the wish of My Father is that His sons should be made perfect like Himself and shine with Him in everlasting glory, rejoicing for ever in His boundless and eternal love.

4. There are little creatures far inferior to man, like the firefly, with its flickering light, and certain small plants among the vegetation in the Himalayas, which by their faint phosphorescent radiance illuminate as far as they can the dark jungle where they live. Tiny fish also that swim in the deep waters of the ocean give forth a glimmering light which guides other fish and helps them to elude their enemies. How much more ought My children to be lights in the world (Matt. v.14) and be eager in self-sacrifice to bring into the way of truth, by means of their God-given light, those who by reason of darkness are liable to become the prey of Satan.

5. If they do not use these heaven-sent powers in the service of God and His creatures they are in danger of losing for ever those heavenly gifts. This is what has happened to certain fish that live in the deep waters of dark caves, also to some hermits in Tibet, for both have lived so long in darkness that they have entirely lost their sight. In like manner the ostrich, through not using its wings, has lost altogether the power of flight. Take heed, therefore, not to neglect whatever gifts or talents have been entrusted to you, but make use of them that you may share in the bliss and glory of your Master (Matt. xxv.14-30).

6. Sometimes when there is some great act of service to be done, I choose for My purpose those who are little esteemed

in the eyes of the world, for they make no boast of their own power or wisdom, but putting their entire trust in Me, and accounting what little ability they possess as of no great value, they devote all they have and are to My work for men (1 Cor. i.26-30). For instance, when I fed in the wilderness five thousand men with five loaves and two fishes, you will remember that I did not perform this miracle by the agency of My disciples, for they were full of doubt and perplexity and wished to send the multitude away hungry (John vi.9). My servant on that occasion was a little lad whom I had cured of the palsy. Filled with a desire to hear My words he determined to follow Me. His poor mother wrapped up in his clothes some barley cakes and dried fish, enough for two or three days journey, so when inquiry was made for food for the multitude this faithful little lad at once brought all that he had and laid it at the disciples' feet. Though there were wealthy people there who had with them much better food, such as wheaten cakes, they were not prepared to give them up; so it was from the barley cakes of this boy, My namesake, that by My blessing the multitude was fed with the choicest food.

7. There are many who are so wanting in gratitude that whatever blessings are bestowed upon them, even to the extent of miracles being performed for their benefit, they still remain dissatisfied and ungrateful. Such people can never be used for the service and blessing of others, but are like the man whom I healed after he had suffered for thirty-eight years from an incurable disease, for instead of being grateful and believing on Me he did not even trouble to remember My name (John v.12-13). From such people the world can hope for no blessing; it comes only from those who, like the poor

widow, are ready to give up all they have, even all their living (Luke xxi.2-4).

8. For true service and the performance of duty My servants must be ready to offer even life itself--like that faithful soldier who remained at his post in the bitter cold and falling snow till he froze to death, and like a statue still kept his place, though the others of the watch went off to warm themselves at the fire. When the king came and saw him standing fixed and faithful still in death, he took off his crown and placed it for a space upon his head, saying: "Such a faithful soldier and servant is worthy of the honour and glory of my diadem. Would that he had lived, for then I would have made him the head of my kingdom!" Such must my faithful servants be in the service to which I have appointed them, and to those who finish their work with like faith and courage I will grant a fadeless crown of eternal kingship (2 Tim. iv.4, 5-8).

9. Many there are who have wasted the precious time given to them for My service, but even now there is an opportunity for them to rouse themselves and make the best use of the time that remains to them. They are like a hunter who, while wandering in the jungle, picked up some pretty stones on the bank of a stream. Unaware of their value he used them one by one in his sling to shoot at the birds seated on the trees near the river, and so one by one they fell into the water and were lost. With one still in his hand he returned to the city, and as he passed along the bazaar a jeweller caught sight of it, and told the silly fellow that it was a valuable diamond for which he could get thousands of rupees. When he heard this he began to bewail himself and say, "Woe is me! I didn't know their value, and have been using many of these diamonds to

shoot at birds by the riverside, and they have fallen into the river and are lost, otherwise I should have been a millionaire. Still I have saved this one, and that is something gained." Every day is like a precious diamond, and though many priceless days have been wasted in the pursuit of fleeting pleasures, and are for ever sunk in the depths of the past, you should awake to the value of what remains, and bringing it into the best possible use gather for yourself spiritual riches. Use it in My service, who have given to you life and all its priceless blessings, and by using them to save others from sin and death you will obtain an everlasting and heavenly reward.

V.
THE CROSS AND THE MYSTERY OF SUFFERING

SECTION I

The Disciple,--
What is the meaning and purpose of the cross, and why do pain and suffering exist in the world?

The Master,--
1. The cross is the key to heaven. At the moment when by My baptism I took the cross upon My shoulders for the sake of sinners, heaven was opened, and by means of My thirty-three years bearing of the cross and by death upon it, heaven, which by reason of sin was closed to believers, was for ever opened to them.

Now as soon as believers take up their cross and follow Me they enter heaven through Me (John x.9) and begin the enjoyment of that unbounded bliss which the world cannot understand, for heaven is closed to unbelief. Hope and experience will teach the unbeliever that joy follows pain, but that that joy does not endure. But I give to My children ease in pain, and perfect happiness and peace. Those who joyfully take up My cross are themselves upborne by it, and ever supported by that cross they enter heaven at last.

2. Pain arises out of man's perverse and rebellious nature, just as tropical heat is irksome and painful to those who live in cold lands, and bitter cold to those who live in tropic climes. Heat and cold depend on the relation of the earth to the sun. So man, by the exercise of his own free will, enters into a state of agreement or disagreement with God, and inasmuch as the laws of God are intended for the spiritual health and happiness of man, opposition to them brings about spiritual pain and suffering. Now God, instead of altogether removing these states of opposition and rebellion to His will, makes use of them to make clear to man that this world was not created to be his home, but is to him a foreign land (2 Cor. v.1,2,6).

This world is but to prepare him for a perfect and eternal home, and the oft-repeated blows of ill-fortune are intended to keep his spirit awake, lest he should become careless, and falling away from the truth share in the ruin of this unstable world. He is meant to come into communion with his Maker and, after being freed from the suffering and misery of this fleeting life, to enter into His heaven of eternal happiness and peace.

3. Pain and suffering are bitter as poison, but it is also well known that sometimes the antidote of a poison is itself a poison. And thus I sometimes employ pain and suffering as bitter medicines in order to promote the spiritual health and vigour of My believers. As soon as their perfect health is secured there will be an end of all suffering. Their pain is no pleasure to Me, for My one object is their eternal well-being (Lam. iii.31,33).

4. Just as after a shock of earthquake springs of sweet water sometimes emerge in desert places, and the arid wastes are irrigated and become fruitful, so in certain cases the shock of suffering opens up within the heart of a man hidden springs of living water, and in place of murmurings and complainings there issue from him streams of gratitude and joy (Ps. cxix.67,71).

5. As soon as a child enters the world it is most necessary that it should begin to cry and scream, so that its breath may have free play and its lungs be brought into full use; and if for some reason it does not cry out it must be slapped till it does so. Just so with perfect love. I sometimes cause My children to cry out by the blows and stings of pain and suffering, that the breath of prayer may have free course through the lungs of their spirit and they may thus gain fresh vigour and abide in endless life.

6. The cross is like a walnut whose outer rind is bitter, but the inner kernel is pleasant and invigorating. So the cross does not offer any charm of outward appearance, but to the cross-bearer its true character is revealed, and he finds in it the choicest sweets of spiritual peace.

7. When I became incarnate, I bore the cruel cross for man's salvation, not for the six hours of My crucifixion only, or even for the three and a half years of My ministry, but for the whole thirty-three and a half years of My life, in order that man might be delivered from the bitterness of death. Just as it is painful to a cleanly man to stay for even a few minutes in a filthy and unclean place, so those who abide in Me find it most distasteful to have to live among vicious people; and this is the reason why some men of prayer, distressed by the

foulness of sin, have abandoned the world and gone to live as hermits in deserts and caves. Consider this, then, when men who have been sinners themselves feel the presence of sin so hard to bear that they cannot endure the company of their own kind, so much that they leave them, and never wish to return to them again, how extremely painful and hard a cross must Mine have been, that I, the Fountain of Holiness, should have had to live for more than thirty-three years constantly among men defiled with sin. To understand this and rightly to appreciate it is beyond the powers of man's mind, and even the angels desire to look into it (1 Pet. i.12). For before the creation they knew that God is Love, and yet it was to them a most wonderful and amazing thing that the love of God should be such that, in order to save His creatures and to bring to them eternal life, He should become incarnate and bear the cruel cross.

8. In this life even I share the cross of those who abide in Me, and enter into their sufferings (Acts ix.4). Though they are creatures and I am their Creator, yet, just as the body and the spirit, though separate entities, are yet so intermingled that if even the smallest part of the body feels pain the spirit immediately becomes conscious of it; so I am the life and spirit of My children, and they are, as it were, My body and members. I share their every pain and grief, and at the right moment give them relief.

9. As I Myself bore the cross I am able to deliver and keep in perfect safety those who are crossbearers, even while they walk amid fires of persecution. I was with the three young men in Nebuchadnezzar's furnace, which with all its raging had no power to hurt them (Dan. iii.23-5; 1 Peter iv.12-13). So those who by the baptism of the Holy Spirit have received

the new life will never feel the fires of persecution nor any hurtful thing, for they ever abide in Me in eternal peace and safety.

SECTION II

1. In the bitter cold of winter the trees stand bare of leaves, and it seems as if their life, too, had departed for ever, yet in the spring time they put forth new leaves and beautiful flowers, and the fruit begins to show itself. So was it with Me in My crucifixion and resurrection, and so it is with my faithful cross-bearers (2 Cor. iv.8-11; vi.4-10). Though they seem to be crushed and dead beneath their cross they still put forth the beautiful flowers and glorious fruits of eternal life which abide for ever.

2. In grafting a sweet tree on to a bitter one, both feel the knife and both are called upon to suffer in order that the bitter may bear sweet fruit. So, too, in order to introduce good into man's evil nature, it was necessary that first of all I Myself and afterwards believers also should suffer the agonies of the cross, that they might in future for ever bear good fruit, and thus the glorious love of God be made manifest.

3. If in this world men persecute and slander you do not let this surprise or distress you, for this is for you no place of rest, but a battlefield. Woe to you when men of the world praise you (Luke vi.26), for this proves that you have taken on their perverse ways and habits. It is against their very nature and temper to praise My children, for light and darkness cannot exist together. If for the sake of appearances evil men act contrary to their nature and cease to persecute you, yours is

the greater injury, for their influence enters into your spiritual life, and your spiritual progress is hindered.

Further, to put your trust in the world or in worldly men is to build your house upon the sand, for today they will raise you aloft and tomorrow will so cast you down that there will be no trace left of you, for they are in all things unstable. When I went up to Jerusalem at the Passover, they all with one voice began to cry out, "Hosanna! Hosanna!" (Matt. xxi.9), and only three days after, when they saw that what I said was against their life of sin and self-seeking, they at once changed over and began to cry, "Crucify Him! Crucify Him!" (Luke xxiii.21).

4. If through some misunderstanding some, or even all, believers turn against you and cause you pain, you must not count it a misfortune, for if in all honesty and faithfulness under the guidance of the Holy Spirit you continue to do your duty, remember that God Himself and all the hosts of heaven are on your side.

Do not allow yourself to be discouraged, for the time is at hand when all your good designs and purposes and all your unselfish love will be made known to the whole world, and, in the presence of all, honour will be done to you for your labours and faithful service.

I, too, for the salvation of men, had to renounce all things, and was Myself renounced by all, yet at the last I regained all and everything. Neither be surprised if the world desert you, for it has deserted God Himself, so that in this you are seen to be a true son of your Father.

5. Do not suppose that those who live in luxury and seem to be always successful in worldly affairs are all true worshippers of God, for the opposite is often the case. It is possible for sheep to wander away from the fold and the shepherd, and find in the jungle good pasturage, but they are all the time in danger of being torn to pieces by wild beasts, which will indeed be their fate in the end. But those who abide in the fold with the shepherd, though they may appear to be sick and feeble, are certainly free from danger and in the shepherd's care. This is the difference between believers and unbelievers.

6. The life of the believer and that of the unbeliever show great similarity in their beginning, but when their end comes, they are as diverse as the snake and the silkworm. The snake, however many times he casts his skin, remains a snake and nothing else, but the silkworm, when it casts off its unsightly cocoon, becomes a new creature, and as a dainty pretty moth flies about in the air. So the believer, casting aside this body, enters into a state of spiritual glory and flies about for ever in heaven, while the sinner after death is but a sinner still.

Though the silkworm, cramped within the cocoon, is in a state of depression and struggle as though upon a cross, yet this very condition of strife and difficulty gives strength to its wings, and fits it for the life that is to be. So My children, while in the body, are in a state of spiritual struggle and conflict, and look forward to their release with sighs and longing, but through the bearing of the cross I give them strength, and they become fully prepared and fitted for that state of endless life (Rom. viii.23).

7. In the midst of this spiritual warfare, and even while they are bearing their cross, I give them a truly wonderful peace of heart, that their courage may not fail. For instance, when a faithful martyr of Mine had borne witness to Me in word and deed, his enemies took him and hung him up to a tree head downwards. In this condition such was his peace of mind that he was utterly unconscious of the pain and disgrace to which he was subjected, and turning to his persecutors said, "The way you have treated me does not distress or dismay me, for I can expect nothing else in a world where everything is upside down, and where one can see nothing upright. In accordance with your own nature you have turned me as you think upside down, but in reality I am right side up. Just as when a slide is put into a magic lantern wrong way up it shows the picture correctly, so though now in the eyes of the world I am upside down, I am for ever right side up before God and the heavenly world, and I praise Him for this glorious cross."

8. For believers it would sometimes be an easy thing to become a martyr to My Name, but I also need living witnesses who will daily offer themselves as living sacrifices for the salvation of others (1 Cor. xv.31). For death is easy, but it is hard to live, for a believer's life is a daily dying. But those who are thus ready to lay down their lives for My sake shall share My glory and live with Me for ever in fullness of joy.

9. Should pain and suffering, sorrow, and grief, rise up like clouds and overshadow for a time the Sun of Righteousness and hide Him from your view, do not be dismayed, for in the end this cloud of woe will descend in showers of blessing on your head, and the Sun of Righteousness rise upon you to set no more for ever (John xvi.20-22).

VI.
HEAVEN AND HELL

The Disciple,--
Master, what are heaven and hell, and where are they?

The Master,--
1. Heaven and hell are the two opposite states in the spiritual realm. They have their origin in the heart of man and it is in this world that their foundations are laid. Since man cannot see his own spirit, so neither can he see these two states of the soul. But he has experience of them within him, just as he feels pain from a blow and perceives sweetness from eating sweetmeats. The wound caused by the blow may increase until it caused the greatest pain and finally ends in death and decay, as on the other hand the sweetmeats may by digestion promote strength. In the same way the pain of a sinful act and the happiness of a good deed may to some extent be apparent immediately, yet the full penalty or reward for them will be perceived only on entry into the spiritual realm.

2. In this world man is never satisfied for long with one thing, but is ever in search of a change of circumstances or surroundings; for which it is clear that the fleeting things of this world never can satisfy him, for he wants something that is stable and unchanging and always agreeable to his tastes and desires. When in his search he finds this reality in Me,

the desire for all further change comes to an end, because one does not grow wearied of perfect society and complete happiness, for this is the one demand of both body and spirit. In truth, to obtain a true peace is the one object of the human soul. Sometimes there comes to the heart of man, without any thought or desire of his own, a sudden sensation of pleasure or pain which is an emanation from the spiritual world of heaven or hell. These come to him again and again, gradually one or other of these prevails, according to his spiritual habit, and by steadily appropriating one of these he makes a final choice. In this way the foundation of heaven or hell is built up in a man's heart while still in this world, and after death he enters into that state which, in this life, his desires or passions have prepared him for.

3. Some say that desire is the root of all pain and sorrow, therefore it is not right to desire happiness in heaven or in communion with God, for salvation consists in killing all desire. To say this is as great a folly as to tell a thirsty man to kill his thirst instead of giving him water to drink, for thirst or desire is part of life itself. To take away desire or thirst without satisfying them is to destroy life, and this is not salvation but death. Just as thirst implies water, and water is intended to remove thirst, so the existence of desire in the soul implies the existence of true happiness and peace. When the soul finds Him who planted within it that desire, it receives far greater satisfaction than the thirsty man does from water, and this satisfaction of the soul's desire we call heaven.

4. There are many in this world who are like the man who died from thirst although he was in the midst of the boundless waters of the ocean, for sea water could not quench his thirst or save his life. Just so there are men who are living

in the boundless ocean of love, and yet because the fresh water of God's grace is bitterness to them in their disobedience and sin, they perish with thirst. But for those who repent of their sin and turn to Me fountains of living water gush up from that sea of love, and they find in Him who loves them satisfaction and enduring peace. This, too, we call heaven.

5. There are many who have conceived such a love and devotion to the world that though by the example and teaching of My children their hearts are often lifted heavenwards, yet drawn down by the force of gravity, like stones that have been thrown upwards, they fall back into the world and finally slip into hell. But when man turns his heart to Me in true repentance, I cleanse the temple of his heart with the whips of love and make it a heavenly abode for the King of kings. This earthly life is such that the glory and pomp of kings are seen but today, and tomorrow are mingled with the dust. But those who become sons of the kingdom of God have glory and honour, thrones and crowns, and of their kingdom, which is heaven, there is no end.

6. Sinners in order to increase their pleasures steal the good things of others, and that is why men, good as well as bad, lock up their houses when they go abroad. And this locking up of goods must go on as long as men's hearts are locked against their Lord and Maker. When, however, the lock of the heart is open to Him whoever stands knocking at the door (Rev. iii.20), the desires and longings of the heart will be fulfilled. Then there will be no further need for the locking up of houses, for instead of stealing each other's goods and doing each other mischief all will serve one another in love. For when men give to God what is due to Him they will seek

only what is good. Thus they enter into His wondrous joy and peace; and this is heaven.

7. When I gave My life upon the cross for the sons of men that I might save sinners from hell and lead them into heaven, two thieves, one on each side of Me, met death at the same time. Although to all appearance we all three suffered a like fate, from a spiritual point of view there was a vast difference. One of them shut up his heart against Me and met his death unrepentant, but the other opened his heart to Me in true repentance, and in communion with Me found life, and that very day entered Paradise with Me (Luke xxiii.39-43). This Paradise exists not only beyond the grave, but begins in the hearts of men now, though it is hidden from the eyes of the world (Luke xvii.21). A faithful martyr of Mine was at the point of death after suffering untold agonies at the hands of his persecutors, and was so filled with the joy of heaven that he turned to them and said, "O that I could open my heart to you, and show you the wonderful peace I have, which the world can neither give nor take away! Then you would be convinced of its truth, but it is the hidden manna which is unseen and unseeable." After his death those foolish folk tore out his heart, hoping to find something precious in it, but they found nothing, for the reality of that heaven is known only to those who accept it and find in it their joy.

8. The womb of Mary, where in a fleshly form I had My abode for a few months, was not a place so blessed as the heart of the believer in which for all time I have My home and make it a heaven (Luke ix.27,28).

9. There are many who long for heaven yet miss it altogether through their own folly. A poor beggar sat for

twenty-one years on the top of a hidden treasure chamber, and was so consumed with the desire to be rich that he horded up all the coppers that he received. Yet he died in a miserable state of poverty, utterly unaware of the treasure over which he had been sitting for years. Because he sat so long on the same spot a suspicion arose that he had something valuable buried there. So the Governor had the place dug up and discovered a hoard of valuables, which afterwards found its way into the royal treasury. My word is nigh thee, in thy mouth and in thy heart (Deut. xxx.14).

10. Those who know nothing of the spiritual life declare that it is impossible to experience real peace and heavenly joy in this grief-stricken world. But those who have experience of the spiritual life know that just as one finds here and there in the midst of the ice fields of the polar regions flowing streams of hot water, so in the midst of this cold and sorrow-laden world there are to be found flowing in the hearts of believers restful streams of heavenly peace, for the hidden fire of the Holy Spirit glows within them.

11. Although God made all men of one blood and created all in His own form and likeness, He has made them to differ in character, temperament, and powers. For if all the flowers in the world were of the same colour and scent, then the very face of the earth would lose its charm. The sun's rays as they pass through coloured glass do not change the colours, but only bring out their varied beauty and charm. In the same way the Sun of Righteousness, both in this world and in heaven, through the God-given virtues of believers and saints continually makes manifest His unbounded glory and love. Thus I abide in them and they in Me, and they will have joy for evermore.

SECTION II

The Disciple,--
Master, some people say that the comfort and joy that believers experience are simply the outcome of their own thoughts and ideas. Is this true?

The Master,--
1. That comfort and abiding peace which believers have within themselves is due to My presence in their hearts, and to the life-giving influence of the fullness of the Holy Spirit. As for those who say that this spiritual joy is the result only of the thoughts of the heart, they are like a foolish man who was blind from his birth, and who in the winter time used to sit out in the sunshine to warm himself. When they asked him what he thought of the sun's heat he stoutly denied that there was such a thing as the sun, and said, "This warmth which I am now feeling on the outside comes from within my own body, and is nothing more than the powerful effort of my own thoughts. This is utter nonsense that people tell me about something like a big ball of fire hanging up in the sky." Take heed, therefore, lest anyone captures you "with philosophy and vain deceit, after the traditions of men and after the rudiments of the world." (Col. ii.8).

2. If true happiness depended on the thoughts of man, then all philosophers and deep thinkers would be filled to overflowing with it. But with the exception of such of them as believe in Me, those who are wise in the philosophy of this world are altogether devoid of happiness, except for a kind of fleeting pleasure which they derive from following out certain rules of their own.

But I have so created man that he has a natural fitness for the reception of the Holy Spirit by means of which alone is he able to receive this heavenly life and joy. As in charcoal there is a natural fitness to receive fire, but without oxygen the fire cannot enter it, so unless the oxygen of the Holy Spirit finds an entrance into a man's soul he will remain in darkness and will never enjoy this true and lasting peace (John iii. 8).

3. This fitness of heart and thoughts of man is like that of the strings of a guitar or violin. When these are tightened and made to harmonize, then by the touch of the plectrum or the bow the most charming music is produced; but if that is not done the touch of the bow only produces discords. And the production of sweet sounds when the strings all harmonize is again dependent on the air, by the force and motion of which sound is carried into the ear. In the same way, to harmonize the thoughts and imaginations of men the presence of the stimulating breath of the Holy Spirit is necessary. When that is present there will be produced heavenly airs and joyous harmonies in men's hearts, both in this life and in heaven.

The Disciple,--
Master, sometimes I am conscious that my peace and happiness have departed. Is this because of some hidden sin of mine, or is there some other reason unknown to me?

The Master,--
1. Yes, this is sometimes due to disobedience, but occasionally I appear to leave My children for a short time and then they become lonely and restless. Then while they are in that condition I am able to reveal to them their actual selves and their utter weakness, and teach them that apart from Me they are nothing but dry bones (Ezek. xxxvii.1-14); so that they

may not in a constant state of rest and peace forget their essential condition, and, deeming themselves to be God, fall through pride into the punishment of hell (1 Tim. iii.6; Jude 6; Isa. xiv. 12-17). In this way they are trained and educated; and when they humbly and meekly abide in Me, who created them, they will enjoy eternal happiness in heaven.

2. Sometimes it happens that when I enter into My children and fill them with the fullness of the Spirit, they overflow with such divine happiness and joy that they are not able to endure the glory and blessing that is theirs, and so fall into a state of faintness or even unconsciousness. For flesh and blood cannot inherit the kingdom of God, nor temporal things those which are eternal, until men are set free from the power of vain mortality and raised into glory (1 Cor. xv. 50,53; Rom. viii. 19-22). Then shall My will be done on earth in every creature, even as it is done in heaven. Then shall pain and suffering, sorrow and sighing, woe and death be for ever done away, and all My children shall enter into the kingdom of My Father, which is joy in the Holy Ghost, and they shall reign for ever and ever (Rom. xiv. 17; Rev. xxi. 4; xxii. 5).

A PRAYER

Dear Master,

Thy varied blessings and gifts have filled my heart to overflowing with gratitude and praise. But the praise of heart and tongue do not suffice me until I prove by my deeds that my life is devoted to Thy service. Thanks and praise be to Thee that Thou hast brought me, unworthy though I am, out of death into life and made me to rejoice in Thy fellowship and love. I know not as I ought either myself or my sore need, but Thou, O Father, knowest full well Thy creatures and their necessities. Nor can I love myself as Thou lovest me. To love myself truly is to love with heart and soul that boundless love which gave me being, and that love Thou art. Thou hast therefore given me but one heart, that it might be fixed on one only, on Thee, who didst create it.

Master, to be seated at Thy feet is better far than to sit upon the lordiest throne of earth, for it means to be enthroned for ever in the eternal kingdom. And now, on the altar of these sacred feet I offer myself as a burnt sacrifice. Graciously accept me, and wheresoever and howsoever Thou wilt, use me for Thy service. For Thou art mine, and I belong to Thee, who didst take this handful of dust and make me in Thine own image and didst grant me the right to become Thy son.

All honour and glory and praise and thanksgiving be unto Thee for ever and ever. Amen.

PUBLISHERS' PREFACE

The life of Sadhu Sundar Singh was most remarkable in it's Christ-likeness. He was born amidst the depths of Indian culture and religion, and into a Sikh family. During the early part of his life, Sundar's mother would take him week by week to sit at the feet of a sadhu, an ascetic holy man, who lived some distance away in the rainforest.

But with the death of his beloved mother when he was only fourteen years old, the young Sundar grew increasingly despairing and aggressive. His hatred of the local missionaries and Christians culminated in the public burning of a bible, which he tore apart page by page and threw, into the flames.
Yet before long Sundar was intent on taking his own life. Sundar had arrived at a point of desperation: he had decided to throw himself under the Ludhiana express if God did not reveal to him the true way of peace.

At three in the morning he rose from his bed and went out into the moonlit courtyard for the ceremonial bath observed by devout Hindus and Sikhs before worship. He then returned to his room and knelt down, bowed his head to the ground and pleaded that God would reveal himself. Yet, nothing happened.

He had not known what to expect: a voice, a vision, and a trance? Still nothing happened. And it was fast approaching the time for the Lothian express.

He lifted his head and opened his eyes, and was rather surprised to see a faint cloud of light in the room. It was too early for the dawn. He opened the door and peered out to the courtyard. Darkness. Turning back into the room, he saw that the light in the room was getting brighter. To his sheer amazement, he saw not the face of any of his traditional gods, but of Jesus the Christ.

Jesus Christ was there in the room, shining, radiating an inexpressible joy, peace, and love, looking at him with compassion and asking, "Why do you persecute me? I died for you..."

From here on the life of Sundar Singh became most Christ-like. Being unwilling to denounce his Master, it was not long before his family had rejected him. Sundar took the saffron robes of the sadhu and began a life of spreading the simple message of love and peace and rebirth through Jesus. He carried no money or other possessions, only a New Testament.

He traveled India and Tibet, as well as the rest of the world, with the message that the modern interpretation of Jesus was sadly watered down. He visited the West twice, traveling to Britain, the United States, and Australia in 1920, and Europe again in 1922.

With the large number of "spiritual paths" and "techniques", facing the world of today it is of special value to consider the life and insights of one who truly embraced the simplicity, love and freedom offered through devotion to Christ.

"I am not worthy to follow in the steps of my Lord," he said, "but like Him, I want no home, no possessions. Like Him I will belong to the road, sharing the suffering of my people, eating with those who will give me shelter, and telling all people of the love of God."

PREFACE by SUNDAR SINGH

The following is the preface of the original publication of 1926:

In this book, I have attempted to write about some of the visions, which God has given me. Had I considered my own inclinations I would not have published the account of these visions during my life time; but friends, whose judgment I value, have been insistent that, as a spiritual help to others, the publication of the teaching of these visions should not be delayed. In deference to the wish of these friends, this book is now presented to the public.

At Kotgarh, fourteen years ago, while I was praying, my eyes were opened to the Heavenly Vision. So vividly did I see it all that I thought I must have died, and that my soul had passed into the glory of heaven; but throughout the intervening years these visions have continued to enrich my life. I cannot call them up at will, but, usually when I am praying or meditating, sometimes as often as eight or ten times in a month, my spiritual eyes are opened to see within the heavens, and, for an hour or two, I walk in the glory of the heavenly sphere with Christ Jesus, and hold converse with angels and spirits. Their answers to my questions have provided much of the material that has already been published in my books, and the unutterable ecstasy of that spiritual communion makes me long for the time when I shall enter in permanently to the bliss and fellowship of the redeemed.

Some may consider that these visions are merely a form of spiritualism, but I would emphasize that there is one very essential difference. Spiritualism does presume to produce messages and signs from spirits out of the dark, but they are usually so fragmentary and unintelligible, if not actually deceptive, that they lead their followers away from, rather than to, the truth. In these visions, on the other hand, I see vividly and clearly every detail of the glory of the spiritual world, and I have the uplifting experience of very real fellowship with the saints, amid the inconceivably bright and beautiful world made visible. It is from these angels and saints that I have received, not vague, broken and elusive messages from the unseen, but clear and rational elucidations of many of the problems that have troubled me.

This "Communion of the Saints" was a fact so real in the experience of the early Church, that it is given a place among the necessary articles of their faith, as stated in the "Apostles' Creed." Once, in a vision, I asked the saints for a proof from the Bible of this communion of saints, and was told that it was to be found clearly given in Zechariah 3:7-8, where "those that were standing by" were not angels, but saints in glory; and God's promise, on condition of Joshua fulfilling His command, is that he will be given "a place of access to walk among them (saints) that stand by," and these are his "fellows" the spirits of men made perfect with whom he could commune. There is repeated mention of Spirits, Saints and Angels in this book. The distinction I would make between them is that spirits are good or bad, which after death exist in a state intermediate between heaven and hell. Saints are those who have passed on through this stage into the higher sphere of the spiritual world, and have had special service allotted to them. Angels are those glorious beings to whom all kinds of superior service have been allotted, and among them are included many saints from other worlds, as well as from this world of ours, who live together as one family. They serve one another in love, and, in the effulgence of God's glory, are eternally happy. The World of Spirits means that intermediary state into which spirits enter after leaving the body. By the Spiritual World is meant all spiritual beings that progress through the stages between the darkness of the bottomless pit and the throne of the Lord in light.

I wish to express my sincere thanks to Rev. T. E. Riddle of the New Zealand Presbyterian Mission, Kharar, Punjab, who has journeyed up to Subathu to translate the original book from Urdu into English. My thanks are again due to Miss E. Sanders, of Coventry, for having corrected the proofs.

SUNDAR SINGH
Subathu, July 1926.

The Visions

LIFE

There is only one source of Life--an Infinite and Almighty Life, whose creative power gave life to all living things. All creatures live in Him and in Him will they remain forever. Again, this Life created innumerable other lives, different in kind, and in the stages of their progress man is one of these, created in God's own image that he might ever remain happy in His holy presence.

DEATH

This life may change but it can never be destroyed, and though the change from one form of existence into another is called Death, this never means that death finally ends life, or even that it adds to life, or takes away from it. It merely transfers the life from one form of existence to another. A thing that disappears from our sight has not thereby ceased to exist. It reappears, but in another form and state.

MAN CAN NEVER BE DESTROYED

Nothing in this whole universe was ever destroyed, nor can it ever be, because the Creator has never created anything for destruction. If He had wished to destroy it, He would never have created it. And if nothing in creation can be destroyed, then how can man be destroyed, who is the crown of creation, and the image of his Creator? Can God Himself destroy His own image, or can any other creature do it? Never! If a man is not destroyed at death then at once the question arises, where will man exist after death, and in what state?

I shall attempt to give a brief explanation from my own visional experiences though it is not possible for me to describe all the things which I have seen in visions of the spiritual world, because the language and illustrations of this world are inadequate to express these spiritual realities; and the very attempt to reduce to ordinary language the glory of the things seen is likely to result in misunderstanding. I have, therefore, had to eliminate the account of all those subtle spiritual occurrences, for which only a spiritual language is adequate, and to take up only a few simple and instructive incidents that will prove profitable to all. And since at some time or other every one will have to enter into this unseen spiritual world it will not be without profit, if we, to some extent, become familiar with it.

WHAT HAPPENS AT DEATH?

One day when I was praying alone, I suddenly found myself surrounded by a great concourse of spirit beings, or I might say that as soon as my spiritual eyes were opened I found myself bowed in the presence of a considerable company of saints and angels. At first, I was somewhat abashed, when I saw their bright and glorious state and compared with them my own inferior quality. But I was at once put at ease by their real sympathy and love-inspired friendliness. I had already had the experience of the peace of the presence of God in my life, but the fellowship of these saints added a new and wonderful joy to me. As we conversed together, I received from them answers to my questions relating to my difficulties about many problems that puzzled me. My first inquiry was about what happens at the time of dying and about the state of the soul after death. I said, ' We know what happens to us between childhood and old age, but we know nothing of what happens at the time of death or beyond the gates of death. Correct information about it can be known only by those on the other side of death, after they have entered the spiritual world. "Can you", I asked, "Give us any information about this?"

To this one of the saints answered! "Death is like sleep. There is no pain in the passing over, except in the case of a few bodily diseases and mental conditions. As an exhausted man is overcome by deep sleep, so comes the sleep of death to man. Death comes so suddenly to many, that it is only with great difficulty that they realize that they have left the material world, and entered this world of spirits. Bewildered by the many new things that they see around them, they imagine that they are visiting some country or city of the physical world, which they have not seen before. It is only when they have been more fully instructed, and realize that their spiritual body is different from their former material body, that they allow that they have, in fact, been transferred from the material world to the realm of spirits."

Another of the saints who was present gave this further answer to my question, "Usually," he said, "at the time of death the body loses its power of feeling. It has no pain, but is simply overcome by a sense of drowsiness. Sometimes in cases of great weakness, or after accident, the spirit departs while the body is still unconscious. Then the spirits of those who have lived without thought of, or preparation for, entering the spiritual world, being thus suddenly transferred into the world of spirits, are extremely bewildered, and in a state of great distress at their fate, so, for a considerable period, they have to remain in the lower and darker planes of the intermediate state. The spirits of these lower spheres often greatly harass people in the world. But the only ones that they can injure are those who are like in mind to themselves, who of their own free will open their hearts to entertain them. These evil spirits, allying themselves with other evil spirits, would do immense harm in the world were it not that God has appointed innumerable angels everywhere for the protection of His people, and of His creation, so that His people are always safe in His keeping."

"Evil spirits can injure only those in the world who are like in nature to themselves, and then they can do it only to a limited extent. They can, indeed, trouble the righteous, but not without God's permission. God sometimes does give to Satan and his angels permission to tempt and persecute His people, that they may emerge from the trial stronger and better, as when He allowed Satan to persecute His servant Job. But from such a trial there is gain rather than loss to the believer."

Another of the saints standing by added in reply to my question, "Many whose lives have not been yielded to God, when about to die, seem to become unconscious; but what actually happens is that when they see the hideous and devilish faces of the evil spirits that have come about them, they become speechless and paralyzed by fear. On the other hand the dying of a believer is frequently the very opposite of this. He is extremely happy for he sees angels and saintly spirits coming to welcome him. Then too, his loved ones, who have died before, are permitted to attend his deathbed, and to conduct his soul to the spiritual world. On entering the world of spirits he at once feels at home for not only are his friends about him, but, while in the world he had long been preparing himself for that Home by his trust in God and fellowship with Him."

After that a fourth saint said, "To conduct the souls of men from the world is the work of angels. Usually Christ reveals Himself in the spiritual world to each one in degrees of glory differing in intensity according to the state of each soul's spiritual development. But in some cases, He Himself comes to a deathbed to welcome His servant and in love dries his tears, and leads him into Paradise. As a child born into the world finds everything provided for its wants, so does the soul, on entering the spiritual world find all its wants supplied."

THE WORLD OF SPIRITS

Once in the course of conversation, the saints gave me this information. "After death the soul of every human being will enter the world of spirits, and every one, according to the stage of his spiritual growth, will dwell with spirits like in mind and in nature to himself, either in the darkness or in the light of glory. We are assured that no one in the physical body has entered into the spiritual world, except Christ and a few saints, whose bodies were transformed into glorious bodies, yet to some it has been granted, that, while still dwelling in the world, they can see the world of spirits, and heaven itself, as in 2 Cor. 12:2, though they themselves cannot tell whether they enter Paradise in the body or in the spirit."

After this conversation, these saints conducted me around and showed me many wonderful things and places. I saw that from all sides thousands upon thousands of souls were constantly arriving in the world of spirits, and that all were attended by angels. The souls of the good had with them only angels and good spirits, who had conducted them from their deathbeds. Evil spirits were not allowed to come near to them, but stood far off and watched. I saw also that there were no good spirits with the souls of the really wicked, but about them were evil spirits, who had come with them from their death-beds, while angels, too, stood by and prevented the evil spirits from giving free play to the spite of their malicious natures in harassing them. The evil spirits almost immediately led these souls away towards the darkness, for when in the flesh, they had consistently allowed evil spirits to influence them for evil, and had willingly permitted themselves to be enticed to all kinds of wickedness.

For the angels in no way interfere with the free will of any soul. I saw there, also, many souls who had lately come into the world of spirits, who were attended by both good and evil spirits, as well as by angels. But before long, the radical difference of their lives began to assert itself, and they separated themselves--the good in character towards the good, and the evil towards the evil.

SONS OF LIGHT

When the souls of men arrive in the world of spirits the good at once separate from the evil. In the world all are mixed together, but it is not so in the spiritual world. I have many times seen that when the spirits of the good--the Sons of Light enter into the world of spirits they first of all bathe in the impalpable air-like waters of a crystal clear ocean, and in this they find an intense and exhilarating refreshment. Within these miraculous waters they move about as if in open air, neither are they drowned beneath them, nor do the waters wet them, but, wonderfully cleansed and refreshed and fully purified, they enter into the world of glory and light, where they will ever remain in the presence of their dear Lord, and in the fellowship of innumerable saints and angels.

SONS OF DARKNESS

How different from these are the souls of those whose lives have been evil. Ill at ease in the company of the Sons of Light, and tormented by the all-revealing light of Glory, they struggle to hide themselves in places where their impure and sin-stained natures will not be seen. From the lowest and darkest part of the world of spirits a black and evil-smelling smoke arises, and in their effort to hide themselves from the light, these Sons of Darkness push down, and cast themselves headlong into it, and from it their bitter wails of remorse and anguish are heard constantly to arise. But heaven is so arranged that the smoke is not seen, nor does the spirits in heaven hear the wails of anguish, unless any of them for some special reason should wish to see the evil plight of those souls in darkness.

DEATH OF A CHILD

A little child died of pneumonia, and a party of angels came to conduct his soul to the world of spirits. I wish that his mother could have seen that wonderful sight, then, instead of weeping, she would have sung with joy, for the angels take care of the little ones with a care and a love that no mother ever could show. I heard one of the angels say to another, "See how this child's mother weeps over this short and temporary separation! In a very few years she will be happy again with her child." Then the angels took the child's soul to that beautiful and light-filled part of heaven, which is set apart for children, where they care for them, and teach them in all heavenly wisdom, until gradually the little ones become like the angels.

After some time this child's mother also died, and her child, who had now become like the angels, came with other angels to welcome the soul of his mother. When he said to her, "Mother, do you not know me? I am your son Theodore," the mother's heart was flooded with joy, and when they embraced one another their tears of joy fell like flowers. It was a touching sight! Then as they walked along together he kept on pointing out, and explaining to her the things around them, and during the time appointed for her stay in the intermediate state, he remained with her, and, when the period necessary for instruction in that world was completed he took her with him to the higher sphere where he himself dwelt.

There, on all sides, were wonderful and joyous surroundings, and unnumbered souls of men were there, who in the world had borne all kinds of suffering for the sake of Christ, and in the end had been raised to this Glorious place of honor. All around were matchless and exceedingly beautiful mountains, springs & landscapes, & in the gardens was abundance of all kinds of sweet fruits & beautiful flowers. Everything the heart could desire was there. Then he said to his mother, "In the World, which is the dim reflection of this real world, our dear ones are grieving over us, but, tell me, is this death, or the real life for which every heart yearns?" The mother said, "Son. This is the true life. If I had known in the world the whole truth about heaven, I would never have grieved over your death. What a pity it is those in the world are so blind! In spite of the fact that Christ has explained quite clearly about this state of glory, and that the Gospels again and again tell of this eternal kingdom of the Father, yet, not only ignorant people, but many enlightened believers as well, still remain altogether unaware of its glory. May God grant that all may enter into the abiding joy of this place!"

DEATH OF A PHILOSOPHER

The soul of a German philosopher entered into the world of spirits and saw from afar the incomparable glory of the spiritual world, and the boundless happiness of its people. He was delighted with what he saw, but his stubborn intellectualism stood in the way of his entering into it, and enjoying its happiness. Instead of admitting that it was real, he argued thus with himself, "There is no doubt at all that I see all this, but what proof is there that it has objective existence, and is not some illusion conjured up by my mind? From end to end of all this scene I will apply the tests of logic, philosophy and science, and then only will I be convinced that it has a reality of its own, and is no illusion." Then the angels answered him, "It is evident from your speech that your intellectualism has warped your whole nature, for as spiritual, and not bodily, eyes are needed to see the spiritual world, so spiritual understanding is necessary to comprehend its reality, and not mental exercises in the fundamentals of logic and philosophy. Your science that deals with material facts has been left behind with your physical skull and brain in the World. Here, only that spiritual wisdom is of use which arises out of the fear and love of God." Then said one of the angels to another, "What a pity it is that people forget that precious word of our Lord, 'Except ye be converted, and become as little children, ye shall in no wise enter into the Kingdom of Heaven' (Matt. 18:3). I asked one of the angels what the end of this man would be, and he replied "If this man's life had been altogether bad, then he would at once have joined the spirits of darkness, but he is not without a moral sense, so for a very long time he will wander blindly round in the dim light of the lower parts of the intermediate state, and keep on bumping his philosophical head, until tired of his foolishness, he repents. Then he will be ready to receive the necessary instruction from the angels appointed for that purpose, and, when instructed, will he be fit to enter into the fuller light of God in the higher sphere."

In one sense the whole of infinite space, filled as it is with the presence of God, who is Spirit, is a spiritual world. In another sense, the World also is a spiritual world, for its inhabitants are spirits clothed with human bodies. But there is yet another world of spirits after they leave the body at death. This is an intermediate state -- a state between the glory and light of the highest heavens, and the dimness and darkness of the lowest hells. In it are innumerable planes of existence, and the soul is conducted to that plane for which its progress in the World has fitted it. There, angels especially appointed to this work, instruct it for a time, that may be long or short, before it goes on to join the society of those spirits -- good spirits in the greater light, or evil spirits in the greater darkness -- that are like in nature and in mind to itself.

UNSEEN HELP

Our relatives and dear ones, and at times the saints as well often come from the unseen world to help and protect us, but the angels always do. Yet they have never been allowed to make themselves visible to us, except at a few times of very special need. By ways unrecognized by us they influence us towards holy thoughts, and incline us towards God and towards good conduct, and God's Spirit, dwelling in our hearts, completes that work for the perfecting of our spiritual life, which they have been unable to accomplish.

The greatness of any one does not depend upon his knowledge and position, nor by these alone can any one be great. A man is as great as he can be useful to others, and the usefulness of his life to others depends on his service to them. Hence, in so far as a man can serve others in love, just so far is he great. As the Lord said, "But whosoever will be great among you let him be your servant" (Matt. 20:26). The joy of all those that dwell in heaven is found in this that they serve one another in love, and thus, fulfilling the object of their lives, they remain forever in the presence of God.

THE CORRECTION OF ERROR

When people earnestly desire to live lives pleasing to God, the readjustment of their views, and the renewal of their lives, begin in this world. Not only does the Spirit of God teach them directly but in the secret chamber of their hearts they are helped by communion with the saints, who, unseen by them are ever at hand to assist them towards the good.

But, as many Christian believers, as well as non-Christian seekers after truth, die while still holding false and partial views of truth, their views are corrected in the world of spirits, provided that they are not obstinately welded to their opinions, and are willing to learn, because neither in this world, nor in the next, does God, or any servant of His, force a man to believe anything against his will.

THE MANIFESTATION OF CHRIST

I saw in a vision the spirit of an idolater on reaching the world of spirits begin at once to search for his god. Then the saints said to him, "There is no god here save the One True God, and Christ, who is His manifestation." At this, the man was a good deal astonished, but being a sincere seeker after truth, he frankly admitted that he had been in error. He eagerly sought to know the correct view of truth, and asked if he might see the Christ. Shortly after this Christ manifested Himself in a dim light to him, and to others who had newly arrived in the world of spirits, because at this stage they could not have endured a full exhibition of His glory, for His glory is so surpassing that even the angels look on Him with difficulty, and cover their faces with their wings (Isaiah 6:9). When He does reveal Himself to any one He takes into account the particular stage of progress to which that soul has attained, so He appears dimly, or in the fuller light of His glory, that the sight of Him may be endured. So, when these spirits saw Christ in this dim but attractive light, they were filled with a joy and peace, which is beyond our power to describe. Bathed in the rays of His life-giving light, and with the waves of His love, which constantly flow out from Him, flowing over them, all their error was washed away. Then with all their hearts, they acknowledged Him as the Truth, and found healing, and, bowing in lowly adoration before Him, thanked and praised Him. And the saints, who had been appointed for their instruction; also rejoiced over them.

A LABOURER AND A DOUBTER

Once I saw in a vision a laboring man arrive in the spirit world. He was in great distress, for in all his life he had given no thought to anything but earning his daily bread. He had been too busy to think of God, or of spiritual things. At the same time he had died another had also died, who was a doubter, obstinate in his opinions. Both were ordered to remain for a long period far down in the world of spirits in a place of darkness. In this, being in distress, they began to cry for help. Saints and angels, in love and sympathy, went to instruct them that they might understand how to become members of the Kingdom of Glory and Light. But in spite of their distress, like many other spirits, they preferred to remain on in their dark abode, for sin had so warped their whole character and nature that they doubted everything. They even looked with suspicion on the angels who had come to help them. As I watched I wondered what their end would be, but, when I asked, the only answer I got was from one of the saints, who said, "God may have mercy on them."

We can form an estimate from the depravity of man's perverted nature from this, that, if an evil report about another goes round, even if it is false, a man whose outlook is distorted by sin will at once accept it as true. If, on the other hand, a good and perfectly true report is received, for example that such and such a man is a devout man, who has done this or that work for the glory of God and for the good of his fellows, then, without hesitation, such a hearer will say, "It is all false. So-and-so must have some motive of his own at the back of it all." Should we ask such a man how he knows that the former case is true and the latter false, and what proof he can give, he will have not the slightest proof to put forward.

All that we can learn from such an attitude of mind is, that, as his mind is tainted with evil he believes evil reports because they fit in with his evil nature, and he thinks good reports are lies because they do not fit in with the evil of his heart. By nature, a good man's attitude is the opposite of this. He is naturally inclined to doubt an evil report, and to believe a good report, because this attitude best fits in with the goodness of his nature. Those who in this world pass their lives in opposition to the will of God will have rest of heart neither in this world nor in the world to come; and, on entering the world of spirits they will feel bewildered and distressed. But those who in this world are conformed to the will or the Lord will be at peace on reaching the next, and will be filled with unspeakable joy, because here is their eternal home, and the kingdom of their Father.

THE JUDGMENT OF SINNERS

Many have the idea that if they sin in secret then none will ever know about it, but it is altogether impossible that any sin should remain hidden forever. At some time or other, it will certainly be known, and the sinner will also receive the punishment he deserves. Also, goodness and truth can never be hidden. In the end they must triumph, though, for a time, they may not be recognized. The following incidents will throw light on the state of the sinner.

A GOOD MAN AND A THIEF

Once in a vision, one of the saints recounted this story to me, "Late one night a godly man had to go a distance to do some necessary work. As he went along, he came upon a thief breaking into a shop. He said to him, 'you have no right to take other people's property, and to cause them loss. It is a great sin to do so.' The thief answered, 'If you want to get out of this safely, then get out quietly. If you don't there will be trouble for you.' The good man persisted in his efforts, and, when the thief would not listen, he began to shout and raised the neighbors. They rushed out to seize the thief, but as soon as the good man began to accuse him, the thief retaliated and accused the good man. 'Oh-yes;' he said, 'you think this fellow is very religious, but I caught him in the very act of stealing.' As there were no witnesses both were arrested, and locked up together in a room, while a police officer and some of his men hid themselves to listen to their conversation. Then the thief began to laugh at his fellow prisoner.

'Look,' he said, 'haven't I caught you nicely? I told you at first to get out or it would be the worse for you. Now we'll see how your religion is going to save you.' As soon as the officer heard this, he opened the door and released the good man with honor and a reward, while he gave the thief a severe beating, and locked him in a prison cell. So, even in this world, there is a degree of judgment between good and bad men, but the full punishment and reward will be given only in the world to come."

SECRET SINS

The following was also related to me in a vision. A man in the secret of his own room was committing a sinful act, and he thought that his sin was hidden. One of the saints said, "How I wish that the spiritual eyes of this man had been open at the time, then he would never have dared to commit this sin." For in that room were a number of angels and saints, as well as some spirits of his dear ones, who had come to help him. All of them were grieved to see his shameful conducts and one of them said, "We came to help him, but now we will have to be witnesses against him at the time of his judgment. He cannot see us, but we can all see him indulging in this sin. Would that this man would repent, and be saved from the punishment to come."

WASTED OPPORTUNITIES

Once I saw in the world of spirits a spirit who, with cries of remorse was rushing about like a madman. An angel said, "In the world this man had many chances of repenting and turning towards God, but whenever his conscience began to trouble him he used to drown its prickings in drink. He wasted all his property, ruined his family, and in the end committed suicide, and now in the world of spirits he rushes frantically about like a mad dog and writhes in remorse at the thought of his lost opportunities. We are all willing to help him, but his own perverted nature prevents him from repenting, for sin has hardened his heart, though the memory of his sin is always fresh to him. In the world, he drank to make himself forget the voice of his conscience, but here there is no possible chance of covering up anything. Now his soul is so naked that he himself, and all the inhabitants of the spiritual world, can see his sinful life. For him, in his sin-hardened state, no other course is possible but that he must hide himself in the darkness with other evil spirits, and so to some extent escape the torture of the light."

A WICKED MAN PERMITTED TO ENTER HEAVEN

Once in my presence a man of evil life entered at death into the world of spirits. When the angel and saints wished to help him he at once began to curse and revile them, and say, "God is altogether unjust. He has prepared heaven for such flattering slaves as you are, and casts the rest of mankind into hell. Yet you call Him Love!" The angels replied, "God certainly is Love. He created men that they might live forever in happy fellowship with Him, but men, by their own obstinacy, and by abuse of their free will have turned their faces away from Him, and have made hell for themselves. God neither casts any one into hell, nor will He ever do so, but man himself, by being entangled in sin, creates hell for himself. God never created any hell."

Just then, the exceedingly sweet voice of one of the high angels was heard from above saying, "God gives permission that this man may be brought into heaven." Eagerly the man stepped forward accompanied by two angels, but when they reached the door of heaven, and saw the holy and light-enveloped place and the glorious and blessed inhabitants that dwell there, he began to feel uneasy. The angels said to him, "See how beautiful a world is this! Go a little farther, and look at the dear Lord sitting on His throne." From the door he looked, and then as the light of the Sun of Righteousness revealed to him the impurity of his sin-defiled life, he started back in an agony of self-loathing, and fled, with such precipitancy, that he did not even stop in the intermediate state of the world of spirits, but like a stone he passed through it, and cast himself headlong into the bottomless pit.

Then the sweet and ravishing voice of the Lord was heard saying, "Look, My dear children, none is forbidden to come here, and no one forbade this man, nor has any one asked him to leave. It was his own impure life that forced him to flee from this holy place, for, 'Except a man be born again he cannot see the kingdom of God' (John 3:3).

THE SPIRIT OF A MURDERER

A man, who some years before had killed a Christian preacher, was bitten by a snake in the jungle, and died. When he entered the world of spirits, he saw good and bad spirits all around him, and because the whole aspect of his soul showed that he was a son of darkness, the evil spirits soon had possession of him, and pushed him along with them towards the darkness. One of the saints remarked, "He killed a man of God by the poison of his anger, and now he is killed by the poison of a snake. The old Serpent, the devil, by means of this man, killed an innocent man. Now, by means of another snake, which is like him, he has killed this man, for 'he was a murderer from the beginning' " (John 8:44).

AND THE SPIRIT OF THE MAN MURDERED

As he was being taken away, one from among the good spirits, who had come to help him, said to him, "I have forgiven you with all my heart. Now can I do anything to help you?" The murderer at once recognized him as the same man whom he had killed some years before. Ashamed and smitten with fear he fell down before him, and at once the evil spirits began to clamor loudly, but the angels who were standing at a distance rebuked and silenced them. Then the murderer said to the man whom he had killed, "How I wish that, in the world, I could have seen your unselfish and loving life as I see it now! I regret that through my blindness, and because your body screened your real spiritual life, I could not then see the inner beauty of your life. Also, by killing, you I deprived many of the blessing and benefit that you would have given them. Now I am forever a sinner in God's sight, and fully deserve my punishment. I don't know what I can do except hide myself in some dark cave, because I cannot bear this light. In it, not only does my own heart make me miserable, but all can see every detail of my sinful life." To this the man who had been murdered replied, "You should truly repent, and turn to God, for if you do there is hope that the Lamb of God will wash you in His own blood, and give you new life that you may live with us in heaven, and be saved frown the torment of Hell."

The murderer said in reply, "There is no need for me to confess my sins for they are open to all. In the world, I could hide them, but not here. I want to live with saints like you in heaven, but when I cannot bear the dimness of the self-revealing light in the world of spirits, then what will be my state in the searching brightness and glory of that light-filled place? My greatest hindrance is that, through my sins, my conscience is so dull and hardened that my nature will not incline towards God and repentance. I seem to have no power to repent left in me. Now there is nothing for it, but that I shall be driven out from here forever. Alas for my unhappy state!" As he said this, fear-stricken, he fell down, and his fellow evil spirits dragged him away into the darkness. Then one of the angels said, "See! There is no need for anyone to pronounce a sentence of doom. Of itself, the life of any sinner proves him guilty. There is no need to tell him, or to put forward witnesses against him. To a certain extent, punishment begins in the heart of every sinner while in the world, but here they feel the full effect of it. And God's arrangement here is such that goats and sheep, that is, sinners and righteous, separate of their own accord.

God created man to live in light, in which his Spiritual health and joy are made permanent forever. Therefore, no man can be happy in the darkness of hell, nor, because of his sin-perverted life, can he be happy in the light. So, wherever a sinner may go he will find himself in hell. How opposite to this is the state of the righteous, who freed from sin, is in heaven everywhere!"

THE SPIRIT OF A LIAR

In the world, there was a man so addicted to lying that it had become second nature to him. When he died and entered the world of spirits, he tried to lie as usual, but was greatly ashamed because even before he could speak, his thoughts were known to all. No one can be a hypocrite there, because the thought of no heart can remain hidden. The soul as it leaves the body bears in it the imprint of all its sin, and its very members become witnesses against it. Nothing can blot out that stain of sin except the blood of Christ. When this man was in the world he regularly tried to distort right into wrong, and wrong into right, but, after his bodily death he learned that there never is, and never can be, a possibility of twisting truth into untruth. He who lies injures and deceives no one but himself, so this man by lying had killed the inner perception to truth, which he had once possessed. I watched him as, inextricably tangled in his own deceit, he turned his face away from the light from above, and hurried away far down into the darkness, where none could see his filthy love of lying, except those spirits who were like in nature to himself.

For Truth is always Truth, and it alone gave this man the sentence of his falseness, and condemned him as a liar.

THE SPIRIT OF AN ADULTERER

I saw an adulterer, who had shortly before arrived in the world of spirits. His tongue was hanging out like a man consumed by thirst, his nostrils were distended, and he beat his arms about as if a kind of fire burned within him. His appearance was so evil and loathsome that I revolted at looking at him. All the accompaniments of luxury and sensuality had been left behind in the world and now, like a mad dog, he ran frantically around, and cried, "Curse on this life! There is no death here to put an end to all this pain. And here the spirit cannot die; otherwise, I should again kill myself, as I did with a pistol in the world in order to escape from my troubles there. But this pain is far greater than the pain of the world. What shall I do?" Saying this he ran towards the darkness, where were many other like-minded spirits, and there disappeared.

One of the saints said "Not only is an evil act sin, but an evil thought, and an evil look is also sin. This sin is not confined only to trafficking with strange women, but excess and animalism in relation to one's wife is also sin. A man and his wife are truly joined together not for sensualism but for mutual help and support, that they with their children may spend their lives in the service of mankind and for the glory of God.

But he who departs from this aim in life is guilty of the adulterer's sin."

THE SOUL OF A ROBBER

A robber died and entered the world of spirits. At first he took no interest in his state, or in the spirits about him, but, as his habit was, he at once set about helping himself to the valuables of the place. But he was amazed that in the spirit world the very things seemed to be speaking and accusing him of his unworthy action. His nature was so perverted that he neither knew the true use of these things nor was he fit to use them rightly. In the World, his passions had been so unbridled, that, for the most trifling cause, he, in his anger, had killed or wounded any who had offended him. Now in the world of spirits, he began to act in the same way. He turned on the spirits, who came to instruct him, as if he would have torn them to pieces, like a savage dog will do even in the presence of its master. On this one of the angels said, "If spirits of this kind were not kept down in the darkness or the bottomless pit, then they would cause immense harm wherever they might go. This man's conscience is so dead, that even after he has reached the world of spirits, he fails to recognize that, by murdering and robbing in the world, he has wasted his own spiritual discernment and life. He killed and destroyed others, but in reality, he has destroyed himself. God alone knows if this man, and those who are like him, will remain in torment for ages or forever."

After this, the angels appointed to the duty took him, and shut him down in the darkness from which he is not permitted to come out. The state of evildoers in that place is so terrible, and so inexpressibly fierce is this torment, that those who see them tremble at the sight. Because of the limitations of our worldly speech, we can only say this, that wherever the soul of a sinner is, always and in every way, there is nothing but pain that ceases not for a moment. A kind of lightless fire burns forever and torments these souls, but neither are they altogether consumed, nor does the fire die out. A spirit who was watching what had just happened said, "Who knows but that in the end this may not be a cleansing flame?" In the dark part of the world of spirits, which is called Hell, there are many grades and planes, and the particular one in which any spirit lives in suffering is dependent on the quantity and character of his sins. In fact God made them all in His own image (Gen. 1:26, 27; Col. 1:15), yet by their connection with sin they have disfigured this image, and have made it unbeautiful and evil. They have, indeed, a kind of spiritual body, but it is exceedingly loathsome and frightful, and if they are not restored by true repentance, and the grace of God, (while on earth), then in this fearful form they must remain in torment forever.

THE STATE OF THE RIGHTEOUS AND THEIR GLORIOUS END

Heaven, or the Kingdom of God, begins in the lives of all true believers in this world. Their hearts are always filled with peace and joy, no matter what persecutions and troubles they may have to endure; for God, who is the source of all peace and life, dwells in them. Death is no death for them, but a door by which they enter forever into their eternal home. Or we may say that though they have already been born again into their eternal kingdom, yet when they leave the body, it is for them, not the day of their death, but their day of birth into the spiritual world, and it is for them a time of superlative joy as the following incidents will make clear.

THE DEATH OF A RIGHTEOUS MAN

An angel related to me how a true Christian, who had wholeheartedly served his Master for thirty years, lay dying. A few minutes before he died God opened his spiritual eyes that, even before leaving the body, he might see the spiritual world and might tell what he saw to those about him. He saw that heaven had been opened for him, and a party of angels and saints was coming out to meet him, and at the door, the Savior with outstretched hand was waiting to receive him. As all this broke upon him, he gave such a shout of joy that those at his bedside were startled. "What a joy it is for me," he exclaimed, "I have long been waiting that I might see my Lord, and go to Him. Oh friends! Look at His face all lighted by love, and see that company of angels that has come for me. What a glorious place it is! Friends, I am setting out for my real home, do not grieve over my departure, but rejoice!" One of those present at his bedside said quietly, "His mind is wandering." He heard the low voice and said, "No, it is not. I am quite conscious. I wish you could see this wonderful sight. I am sorry it is hidden from your eyes. Good-bye, we will meet again in the next world." Saving this he closed his eyes, and said, "Lord I commend my soul into thy hands" and so fell asleep.

COMFORTING HIS DEAR ONES

As soon as his soul had left his body the angels took him in their arms, and were about to go off to heaven, but he asked them to delay a few minutes. He looked at his lifeless body, and at his friends, and said to the angels, "I did not know that the spirit after leaving the body could see his own body and his friends. I wish my friends could see me, as well as I can see them, then these would never count me as dead, nor mourn for me as they do." Then he examined his spiritual body and found it beautifully light and delicate, and totally different from his gross material body. On that, he began to restrain his wife and children who were weeping and kissing his cold body. He stretched out his delicate spiritual hands, and began to explain to them, and with great love to press them away from it, but they could neither see him, nor hear his voice, and, as he tried to remove his children from off his body, it seemed as if his hands passed right through their bodies, as if they were air, but they felt nothing at all. Then one of the angels said, "Come, let us take you to your everlasting home. Do not be sorry for them. The Lord Himself, and we also, will comfort them. This separation is but for a few days."

Then in company with the angels he set out for heaven. They had gone forward only a little way when another band of angels met them with cries of "Welcome." Many friends and dear ones, who had died before him, also met him, and on seeing them, his joy was further increased. On reaching the gate of heaven, the angels and saints stood in silence on either side. He entered, and in the doorway was met by Christ. At once, he fell at His feet to worship Him, but the Lord lifted him up, embraced him, and said, "Well done, good and faithful servant, enter thou into the joy of thy Lord At that the man's joy was indescribable. From his eyes tears of joy began to flow, the Lord in great love wiped them away, and to the angels He said, "Take him to that most glorious mansion that, from the beginning, has been prepared for him." Now the spirit of this man of God still held the earthly idea, that to turn his back on the Lord as he went off with the angels would be a dishonor to Him. He hesitated to do this, but, when at last he turned his face towards the mansion, he was astonished to see that wherever he looked he could see the Lord. For Christ is present in every place, and is seen everywhere by saints and angels.

In addition to the Lord, he was delighted to see that on every side there were surroundings that filled him with joy, and that those who are lowest in rank meet without envy those who are higher, and that those whose position is more exalted count themselves fortunate to be able to serve their brethren in lower positions because this is the kingdom of God, and of love.

In every part of heaven, there are superb gardens, which all the time produces every variety of sweet and luscious fruit, and all kinds of sweet scented flowers that never fade. In them creatures of every kind, give praise to God unceasingly. Birds, beautiful in hue, raise their sweet songs of praise, and such is the sweet singing of angels and saints that on hearing their songs a wonderful sense of rapture is experienced.

Wherever one may look there is nothing but scenes of unbounded joy.

This, in truth, is the Paradise that God has prepared for those that love Him, where there is no shade of death, nor error, nor sin, nor suffering, but abiding peace and joy.

THE MANSIONS OF HEAVEN

Then I saw a man of God examining his appointed mansion from a great distance. When this man, in company with the angels, arrived at the door of his appointed mansion, he saw written on it in shining letters the word "Welcome," and from the letters themselves "Welcome, Welcome," in audible sound was repeated and repeated again. When he had entered his home, to his surprise he found the Lord there before him. At this, his joy was more than we can describe, and he exclaimed, "I left the Lord's presence and came here at His command, but I find that the Lord Himself is here to dwell with me." In the mansion was everything that his imagination could have conceived, and everyone was ready to serve him. In the near-by houses, saints, like-minded to himself, lived in happy fellowship. For this heavenly house is the kingdom, which has been prepared for the saints from the foundation of the world (Matt. 25:34), and this is the glorious future that awaits every true follower of Christ.

A PROUD MINISTER AND A HUMBLE WORKMAN

A minister who looked on himself as an exceedingly learned and religious man died at a ripe old age. And without doubt, he was a good man. When the angels came to take him to the place appointed for him by the Lord in the world of spirits, they brought him into the intermediate state, and left him there with many other good spirits, who had lately arrived, in charge of those angels who are appointed to instruct good souls, while they themselves went back to usher in another good spirit. In that intermediate heaven, there are grades upon grades right up to the higher heavens, and the grade into which any soul is admitted for instruction, is determined by the real goodness of his life on earth.

When the angels, who had put this minister in his grade, came back conducting in the other soul, for whom they had gone, they brought him up beyond the grade in which the minister was, on their way up to a higher plane. Seeing this the minister in a blustering voice called out, "What right have you to leave me half-way up to that glorious country, while You take this other man away up near to it? Neither in holiness, nor in anything else, am I in any way less than this man, or than you yourselves." The angels replied, "There is no question here of great or small, or of more or less, but a man is put into whatever grade he has merited by his life and faith. You are not quite ready yet for that upper grade, so you will have to remain here for a while, and learn some of the things that our fellow-workers are appointed to teach. Then, when the Lord commands us, we will, with great pleasure, take you with us to that higher sphere." He said, "I have been teaching people all my life about the way to reach heaven. What more have I to learn? I know all about it."

Then the instructing angels said, "They must go up now, we can't detain them, but we will answer your question. My friend, do not be offended if we speak plainly, for it is for your good. You think you are alone here, but the Lord is also here though you cannot see Him. The pride that you displayed when you said, 'I know all about it' prevents you from seeing Him, and from going up higher. Humility is the cure for this pride. Practice it and your desire will be granted." After this, one of the angels told him, "The man who has just been promoted above you, was no learned or famous man. You did not look at him very carefully. He was a member of your own congregation. People hardly knew him at all, for he was an ordinary working man, and had little leisure from his work. But in his workshop, many knew him as an industrious and honest worker. All who came in contact with him recognized his Christian character. In the war, he was called up for service in France. There, one day, as he was helping a wounded comrade, he was struck by a bullet and killed.

Though his death was sudden, he was ready for it, so he did not have to remain in the intermediate state as long as you will have to do. His promotion depends, not on favoritism, but on his spiritual worthiness. His life of prayer and humility, while he was in the world, prepared him to a great extent for the spiritual world. Now he is rejoicing at having reached his appointed place, and is thanking and praising the Lord, who, in His mercy, has saved him, and given him eternal life."

HEAVENLY LIFE

In heaven, no one can ever be a hypocrite, for all can see the lives of others as they are. The all-revealing light which flows out from the Christ in Glory makes the wicked in their remorse try to hide themselves, but it fills the righteous with the utmost joy to be in the Father's kingdom of Light. There, their goodness is evident to all, it ever increases more and more, for nothing is present that can hinder their growth, and everything that can sustain them is there to help them. The degrees of goodness reached by the soul of a righteous man is known by the brightness that radiates from his whole appearance; for character and nature show themselves in the form of various glowing rainbow-like colors of great glory. In heaven, there is no jealousy. All are glad to see the spiritual elevation and glory of others, and, without any motive of self seeking, try, at all times, truly to serve one another. All the innumerable gifts and blessings of heaven are for the common use of all. No one out of selfishness ever thinks of keeping anything for himself, and there is enough of everything for all. God, who is Love, is seen in the person of Jesus sitting on the throne in the highest heaven. From Him, who is the "Sun of Righteousness," and the "Light of the World," healing and life-giving rays and waves of light and love are seen flowing out through every saint and angel, and bringing to whatever they touch vitalizing and vivifying power. There is in heaven neither east or west, nor north nor south, but for each individual soul or angel, Christ's throne appears as the center of all things.

There also are found every kind of sweet and delicious flower and fruit, and many kinds of spiritual food. While eating them an exquisite flavor and pleasure are experienced but after the are assimilated, a delicate scent, which perfumes the air around, exudes from the pores of the body.

In short, the will and desires of all the inhabitants of heaven are fulfilled in God, because in every life God's will is made perfect, so under all conditions, and at every stage of heaven, there is for every one an unchanging experience of wonderful joy and blessedness.

THE AIM AND PURPOSE OF CREATION

A few months ago, I was lying alone in my room suffering acutely from an ulcer in my eye. The pain was so great that I could do no other work, so I spent the time in prayer and intercession. One day I had been thus engaged for only a few minutes, when the spiritual world was opened to me, and I found myself surrounded by numbers of angels. Immediately I forgot all my pain, for my whole attention was concentrated on them. I mention below a few other subjects on which we conversed together.

NAMES IN HEAVEN

I asked them, "Can you tell me by what names you are known?" One of the angels replied, "Each of us has been given a new name, which none knows except the Lord and the one who has received it (Rev. 2:17). All of us here have served the Lord in different lands and in different ages, and there is no need that any know what our names are. Nor is there any necessity that we should tell our former earthly names. It might be interesting to know them, but what would be the use of it? And then we do not want people to know our names, lest they should imagine us great and give honor to us, instead of to the Lord, who has so loved us that He has lifted us up out of our fallen state, and has brought us into our eternal home, where we will forever sing praises in His loving fellowship - - and this is the object for which He has created us."

SEEING GOD

I asked again, "Do the angels and saints who live in the highest spheres of heaven, always look on the face of God? And, if they see Him, in what form and state does He appear?" One of the saints said, "As the sea is full of water, so is the whole universe filled with God, and every inhabitant of heaven feels His presence about him on every side. When one dives under water, above and below and round about there is nothing but water, so in heaven is the presence of God felt. And just as in the water of the sea, there are uncounted living creatures, so in the Infinite Being of God His creatures exist. Because He is Infinite, His children, who are finite, can see Him only in the form of Christ. As the Lord Himself has said, "He that hath seen Me hath seen the Father" (John 14:9). In this world of spirits, the spiritual progress of any one governs the degree to which he is able to know and feel God; and the Christ also reveals His glorious form to each one according to his spiritual enlightenment and capacity. If Christ were to appear in the same glorious light to-the dwellers of the darkened lower spheres of the spiritual world, as he; appears to those in the higher planes, then they would not be able to bear it. So He tempers the glory of His manifestation to the state of progress, and to the capacity, of each individual soul."

Then another saint added, "God's presence can indeed be felt and enjoyed but it cannot be expressed in words. As the sweetness of the sweet is enjoyed by tasting, and not by the most graphic descriptive phrasing, so every one in heaven experiences the joy of God's presence, and every one in the spiritual world knows that his experience of God is real, and has no need that any should attempt to help him with a verbal description of it."

DISTANCE IN HEAVEN

I asked, "How far from one another are the various heavenly spheres of existence? If one cannot go to stay in other spheres is he permitted to visit them?" Then one of the saints said, "The place of residence is appointed for each soul in that plane to which his spiritual development has fitted him, but for short periods he can go to visit other spheres. When those of the higher spheres come down to the lower, a kind of spiritual covering is given to them, that the glory of their appearance may not be disconcerting to the inhabitants of the lower and darker spheres. So when one from a lower sphere goes to a higher, he also gets a kind of spiritual covering that he may be able to bear the light and glory of that place."

In heaven distance is never felt by any one, for as soon as one forms the wish to go to a certain place he at once finds himself there.

Distances are felt only in the material world. If one wishes to see a saint in another sphere, either he himself is transported there in a moment of thought, or at once, the distant saint arrives in his presence.

THE WITHERED FIG TREE

I inquired of them, "Everything is created for some purpose, but it sometimes appears that that purpose is not fulfilled, for instance, the purpose of the fig tree was to produce fruit, but, when the Lord found it fruitless, He withered it up. Can you enlighten me as to whether its purpose was fulfilled or not?" A saint replied, "Undoubtedly its purpose was fulfilled, and was fulfilled more fully. The Lord of Life gives life to every creature for a certain specific purpose, but if that purpose is not fulfilled, He has power to take back the life in order to fulfill some higher purpose. Many thousands of God's servants have sacrificed their lives in order to teach and uplift others. By losing their lives for others, they have helped them, and thus fulfilled the higher purpose of God. And if it is lawful, and a most noble service, for man, who is higher than fig trees and all other created things, to give his life for other men, then how can it be unjust if a mere tree gives its life for the teaching and warning of an erring nation? So through this fig tree Christ taught this great lesson to the Jews, and to the whole world, that those whose lives are fruitless, and who fail in the purpose for which God created them, will be altogether withered and destroyed."

And the facts of history make it abundantly plain to us that the bigoted and narrow Jewish national life of that day was, because of its barrenness, withered away like the fig tree. And in the same way the fruitless lives of others, though outwardly they may appear fruitful, are a cause of deception to others, and will be cursed and destroyed. If any one should object that when the Lord cursed this fig tree, it was not the fruit season and figs should not have been looked for, then he should reflect that for doing good there is no fixed season, because all seasons and times are equally appointed for good works, and that he himself should make his life fruitful and thus fulfill the purpose for which he was created.

IS MAN A FREE AGENT?

Again I asked, "Would it not have been far better if God had created man and all creation perfect, for then man could neither have committed sin, nor because of sin would there have been so much sorrow and suffering in the world; but now, in a creation made subject to vanity, we have all kinds of suffering to undergo?"

An angel who had come from the highest grades of heaven, and occupied a high position there, replied, "God has not made man like a machine, which would work automatically; nor has He fixed his destiny as in the case of the stars and planets, that may not move out of their appointed course, but He has made man in His own image and likeness, a free agent, possessed of understanding, determination, and power to act independently, hence he is superior to all other created things. Had man not been created a free agent he would not have been able to enjoy God's presence, nor the joy off heaven, for he would have been a mere machine, that moves without knowing or feeling, or like the stars that swing unknowingly through infinite space. But man, being a free agent, is by the constitution of his nature, opposed to this kind of soulless perfection -- and a perfection of this kind would really have been imperfection -- for such a man would have been a mere slave whose very perfection had compelled him to certain acts, in the doing of which he could have had no enjoyment, because he had no choice of his own. To him there would be no difference between a God and a stone."

Man, and with him all creation, has been subjected to vanity but not forever. By his disobedience, man has brought himself, and all other creatures, into all the ills and sufferings of this state of vanity. In this state of spiritual struggle alone can his spiritual powers be fully developed, and only in this struggle can he learn the lesson necessary to his perfection. Therefore, when man at last reaches the state of perfection of heaven, he will thank God for the sufferings and struggle of the present world, for then he will fully understand that all things work together for good to them that love God (Rom. 8:28).

THE MANIFESTATION OF GOD'S LOVE

Then another of the saints said, "All the inhabitants of heaven know that God is Love, but it had been hidden from all eternity that His love is so wonderful that He would become man to save sinners, and for their cleansing would die on the Cross. He suffered thus that He might save men, and all creation, which is in subjection to vanity. Thus God, in becoming man, has shown His heart to His children, but had any other means been used His infinite love would have remained forever hidden. "Now the whole creation, with earnest expectation, awaits the manifestation of the sons of God, when they shall be again restored and glorified. But, at present, they, and all creation, will remain groaning and travailing till this new creation comes to pass. And those also who have been born again groan within themselves, waiting for the redemption of the body; and the time approaches when the whole creation, being obedient to God in all things, will be freed from corruption, and from this vanity forever. Then will it remain eternally happy in God, and will fulfill in itself the purpose for which it was created. Then God will be all in all" (Rom. 8:18-23).

The angels also conversed with me about many other matters, but it is impossible to record them, because, not only is there in the world no language, no simile, by which I could express the meaning of those very deep spiritual truths, but also they did not wish me to attempt it, for no one without spiritual experience can understand them, so in that case, there is the fear that, instead of their being a help, they would be to many a cause of misunderstanding and error. I have, therefore, written only a few of the simplest of the matters talked over, in the hope that from them many may get direction and warning, teaching and comfort. Also, that time is not far distant when my readers will pass over into the spiritual world, and see these things with their own eyes. But before we leave this world forever, to go to our eternal home, we must with the support of God's grace, and in the Spirit of prayer, carry out with faithfulness our appointed work. Thus, shall we fulfill the purpose of our lives, and enter without any shade of regret, into the eternal joy of the Kingdom of our Heavenly Father.